BE GOOD
and
DO GOOD

BE GOOD
and
DO GOOD

*Thinking Through
Moral Theology*

Bernard V. Brady

ORBIS BOOKS
Maryknoll, New York 10545

ORBIS BOOKS
Maryknoll, New York 10545

Fathers and Brothers
MARYKNOLL™

Founded in 1970, Orbis Books endeavors to publish works that enlighten the mind, nourish the spirit, and challenge the conscience. The publishing arm of the Maryknoll Fathers and Brothers, Orbis seeks to explore the global dimensions of the Christian faith and mission, to invite dialogue with diverse cultures and religious traditions, and to serve the cause of reconciliation and peace. The books published reflect the views of their authors and do not represent the official position of the Maryknoll Society. To learn more about Maryknoll and Orbis Books, please visit our website at www.maryknollsociety.org.

Copyright © 2014 by Bernard V. Brady

Published by Orbis Books, Maryknoll, New York 10545–0302.

Manufactured in the United States of America.

Library of Congress Cataloging-in-Publication Data

Brady, Bernard V. (Bernard Vincent), 1957–
    Be good and do good : thinking through moral theology /
Bernard V. Brady.
        pages   cm
    Includes bibliographical references and index.
    ISBN 978-1-62698-099-0
    1. Christian ethics.   I. Title.
BJ1261.B73 2014
241—dc23

                                        2014006598

For my grandson
Nolan Bernard Brady

Contents

Acknowledgments

Thank you to the good people at Orbis Books for all their work and for their support of this project. To my many students over the years who had to listen as I thought through the fundamentals of moral theology, thank you. I want to particularly thank Laura Margarit, Gina Bugliosi, and Jeff Duresky for their reviews of the manuscripts. The title of the book comes from something I said to my children, Mark, Patrick, Ned, and Ellen (now all adults) as I dropped them off at school for so many years so many years ago, "Be good, do good. Love you, dove you. Have fun and learn a lot." Thank you for being good and doing good, enjoying life and pursing learning. Megan, you seemed to pick all this up without me telling you every day! You must have good parents! And Cindy, I love you.

Acknowledgments

INTRODUCTION

Moral Theology

The joys and the hopes, the griefs and the anxieties of the people of this age, especially those who are poor or in any way afflicted, these are the joys and hopes, the griefs and anxieties of the followers of Christ. —Second Vatican Council, *Gaudium et Spes*

"Teacher, which commandment in the law is the greatest?" He said to him, "'You shall love the Lord your God with all your heart, and with all your soul, and with all your mind.' This is the greatest and first commandment. And a second is like it: 'You shall love your neighbor as yourself.'" —Matthew 22:36–40

The objective of this book is to discuss morality within the context of Christian life and thought. That is to say, this is a book on moral theology. As I begin, I am reminded of G. K. Chesterton's famous quote: "The Church is a house with a hundred gates; and no two men enter at exactly the same angle."[1] Chesterton's quote applies as much to moral theology as it does to the church. There are many ways to "enter" moral theology and many "angles" from which to examine moral theology. This book has a particular approach. Its aim is to reflect on, in a simple and direct way, the fundamentals of moral theology. The book takes seriously the variety of sources for this reflection. It builds from the notions that persons are individuals as well as participants in relationships. It acknowledges the validity of experience, personal and communal, as well as the voice of recognized authorities. This is not a book on moral problems. It is a book that seeks to invite discussion of the things to think about as one thinks about moral problems. As an introduction, it leaves some things aside while making the claim that other things are essential.

The book rests on the assumption that there is something called "morality" that every person, in one way or another, experiences. While this assumption is not controversial, defining what one means

1

by morality has always been the source of controversy. For our purposes, morality is understood as *a set of expectations about persons' behavior and character aimed to enhance the flourishing of persons, their relationships, their communities, and their environments*. Morality is for humans and about humans in their many and complex relationships.

The first quotation above from *Gaudium et Spes* captures the essential link between moral theology and morality in general. Moral theology claims hold of the full range of human experience and is tied to a realistic sense of persons and their lives. Moral theology is, moreover, about personhood within the context of Christian faith and tradition. This context matters. First, morality in this sense is fundamentally a response to God's actions and God's gifts in our lives. Second, moral theology has distinctive sources of authority. The Christian story, by which I mean the Bible and Christian tradition, plays a significant and directive role in moral theology. This role is both descriptive and normative. These sources help us to make sense of ourselves as moral persons (in a descriptive way) and they direct our moral senses as persons (in a normative way). To say that the Christian story plays a significant and directive role in moral theology is not to say that it alone determines moral theology. Any source that helps us understand the nature of personhood and human flourishing is welcome.

Clusters of Ideas in Moral Theology

The particular gate or angle for entering moral theology in this book is the idea that there are seven "clusters" of ideas in moral theology. By this I mean that there are seven sets of ideas or moral experiences that are necessary to understand the whole of moral theology. The first cluster of ideas concerns the way people normally *talk about morality*. I suggest that there are four characteristic forms of moral discourse: narrative, prophetic, ethical, and policy. These will be discussed in chapter 1. Each of us have learned morality and have talked about moral issues through one or more of these forms.

The second cluster of ideas captures the ways persons experience themselves as "being free." I propose four ways *people experience freedom*: freedom from the interference of others, freedom for simple goods, freedom for complex goods, and fundamental freedom. Any consideration of morality is dependent on the sense of freedom experienced by persons. The forms of freedom will be discussed in chapter 2.

The third cluster is the set of particular terms people use in discussing morality. The book suggests that there are four *fundamental moral concepts*: rights, rules, intentions/goals, and virtues. When we talk about morality, these are the terms we use to organize our thoughts. Each of us has probably used all four at one time or another. Chapter 2 will address these terms and their place in moral thinking.

The fourth cluster of ideas describes the process of rational justification in moral theology. I suggest that moral theology has a *distinctive structure* of four parts: theology, anthropology, morality, and appropriation. Notice that morality here appears third in the list. This illustrates two things. First, there are things that "come before" morality, that is to say, reasons and particular worldviews or ideas held by the person (here referred to as theology and anthropology). Second, there are things that "come from" morality, that is to say, particular actions (referred to here as appropriation). Put simply, one's moral view is based on some sort of reasoning and one's moral view is expressed in particular ways of being. This is addressed in chapter 3.

The fifth cluster of ideas concerns the *experience of loving and being loved*. It is common knowledge that love is central to Christian life. The greatest commandments described in the New Testament are to love God and to love your neighbor as yourself. Love is at the foundation of moral theology. Chapter 3 describes essential elements of love, both loving and being loved. Love is affective, affirming, responsive, unifying, and steadfast. I note that justice serves as the "eyes of love" as it directs our sense of who and how to love.

The sixth cluster of ideas concerns how we reflect on particular actions; or, better stated, the *moral meaning of a particular action*. The book suggests four elements that must be considered to understand the moral meaning of an action: the act, the intention, the circumstances, and the life narrative of the person. This is the subject of chapter 4.

The seventh cluster of ideas is the variety of ways people experience their consciences. I suggest that *people experience conscience in four ways*: as a place, a process, a source of feelings, and as an impulse or "voice." We are not only responsible for following our conscience (in these four areas), but we are also responsible for forming our conscience (in these four areas).

Moral Theology and Moral Identity

There are several reasons to study moral theology. Certainly, gaining insight into moral ideas is an important reason, but not the primary one. Moral theology has personal objectives that outweigh the theoretical objectives. The study of moral theology ought to help persons develop a sense of their moral identity, and it ought to guide persons in the development of their moral identity.

"Moral identity" is a term more commonly used in psychology than theology.[2] In psychology, the idea addresses the reality that people frequently do things they know they should not do. Stated differently, it is the sense that one has as a moral person. According to psychologist Tonia Bock, moral identity is "the degree to which moral concerns (i.e., justice, caring, generosity) are a central part of one's identity (i.e., your sense of who you are)."[3] Persons have more or less moral identity. In other words, they can have stronger or weaker experiences of the "unity between their sense of morality and their personal goals."[4] Let me ask you a question about moral identity. On the balance of things, do you prize love, friendship, truth, and care over good looks, being popular, having fun, and wealth?

Your moral identity develops through your life; yet at the same time, for most of us, there is a consistency. Your moral identity is a source of motivation for your actions and gives you a sense of purpose in your life. Some psychologists suggest that persons have particular moral schemas that direct their choices. They have "a mental image of what it means to be a moral person"[5] that mediates their thoughts and feelings on one hand, and their behavior on the other. You may indeed have an image, for example, of what it means to be a good person, a good friend, a good husband, or a good wife, who functions in this way for you.

While psychologists discuss how to measure moral identity and how context informs the development of it (for example, they ask, is moral identity primarily formed in childhood or adolescence?), I am more interested in helping you think about your moral identity. This book is based on the idea that you can develop and nurture your moral identity throughout life. The clusters of ideas discussed in the book can be seen as pieces of your moral identity, elements of the moral schemas that direct your life.

Thus the invitation of this book is twofold. The first is theoretical: An objective of this book is to help you understand some of the foundational elements in moral theology. The second invitation is personal: This book aims to encourage you to think about the elements of your moral identity and how you might want to develop your moral identity in the future.

CHAPTER ONE

How People Talk about Morality

*Bless the L*ORD*, O my soul.*
*O L*ORD *my God, you are very great . . .*

You make springs gush forth in the valleys;
they flow between the hills,
giving drink to every wild animal;
the wild asses quench their thirst . . .
The earth is satisfied with the fruit of your work.

You cause the grass to grow for the cattle,
and plants for people to use,
to bring forth food from the earth,
and wine to gladden the human heart,
oil to make the face shine,
and bread to strengthen the human heart . . .

People go out to their work
and to their labor until the evening.
*O L*ORD*, how manifold are your works!*
In wisdom you have made them all;
the earth is full of your creatures.
*May the glory of the L*ORD *endure forever;*
*may the L*ORD *rejoice in his works.*
　　　　　　　　　　　　　　　　—Psalm 104

There are five ways I can get to work. I can drive. I can get a ride. I can take the #63 bus. I can ride a bike. I can walk. All five ways have pluses and minuses, but they all get me to work. I prefer to ride my bike in good weather and get a ride in bad weather. (Having a variety of options can cause trouble. One day I drove to work and took the bus home!). The way people talk about morality is a little like my example of getting to work. People have different methods to get to the same end. When some people talk about morality, they tell stories. Others offer passionate claims and strong moral stands. Still others prefer rationality to emotion and expect clear reasons and justifications for moral claims. Finally, we have the practical and pragmatic types, who are more interested in what good they can actually do than speaking in moral platitudes.

But there is more to my choice on how I will get to work than at first appears. My decision can reflect deeper issues and motivations. Indeed, I am communicating things to others by my choice. When I ride my bike or when I walk, you probably get the message (without my directly saying it) that I am trying to get some exercise. When I carpool or take the bus instead of driving, you might see that I am trying to reduce my carbon output and my use of a non-renewable resource. When I drive, I am a normal American. There is something similar going on in our choice of how we talk about morality. The choice, to paraphrase poet Robert Frost, "makes all the difference."

The person inclined to tell narratives to communicate morality hopes to reach out to you on a personal and experiential level. She hopes you can relate to the story. She hopes to influence you on a basic human level of empathy. The person who is "out there" on moral issues, the one who has the bumper stickers and strong opinions about what is right and wrong—and tells everyone, hopes her passion is contagious and you will catch it. She hopes to connect with you on a fundamental level of right and wrong. There is no ambiguity here; can't you see this? The third type of person, in somewhat of a reaction to the first two, is more interested in taking the time to intellectually work things out in her mind before jumping into the fold. This person needs to ask the question, "Why?" She demands, "Give me a reason!" This final type is the practical and efficient moralist. She wants to answer "What can we do?" She can get frustrated hearing persons speaking in the other three types. They seem merely to "talk," "yell," and "intellectualize" when there are simple, direct, and effective things that need to be done.

There are, then, four forms of moral discourse: four characteristic ways people communicate morality. You are probably more comfortable with one over the others. In short order, the forms are:

- ◆ Narrative—the speaker as Storyteller;

- ◆ Prophetic—the speaker as Preacher;

- ◆ Ethics—the speaker as Voice of Reason;

- ◆ Policy—the speaker as Lawyer.

This chapter will consider each in turn, and through each we will begin to think about the fundamentals of moral theology. The term "moral theology" is used throughout this book to indicate systematic thinking about morality from a Christian perspective. The primary but not exclusive source for moral theology is the Bible. Moral theology also includes attention to the recognized authorities from the Christian tradition, as well as to contemporary Christian reflection. Given the theological notion that God's creation is good, moral theology also relies on insights into the human condition from other sources, for example philosophy, the sciences, and basic human experience.

The Storyteller: Narrative Discourse

When a great crowd gathered and people from town after town came to him, he said in a parable, "A sower went out to sow his seed. . . . "

Jesus replied, "A man was going down from Jerusalem to Jericho. . . . "

Then he told them a parable, "The land of a rich man produced abundantly. . . . "

Then Jesus said, "There was a man who had two sons. . . . "

Then Jesus said to the disciples, "There was a rich man who had a manager and charges were brought to him that this man was squandering his property. . . . "

"There was a rich man who was dressed in purple and fine linen and who feasted sumptuously every day. . . . "

He said, "In a certain city there was judge who neither feared God nor had respect for people. . . . "

"Two men went up to the temple to pray, one a Pharisee and the other a tax collector. . . . "

So he said, "A nobleman went to a distant country to get royal power for himself and then return. . . . "

—Luke 8:4, 10:30, 12:16, 15:11, 16:1, 16:19,
18:2, 18:10, 19:12

The above passage captures how important parables were in Jesus' teaching. Jesus was a storyteller; much of his teaching was done through narratives. This is an important and often overlooked fact in studying moral theology. But Jesus was not unique here; many people before and after him used stories to engage others in conversations about morality. Indeed, all morality begins in some way with a narrative.

Narratives are central to our lives and basic to our communication with other people. For example, if I were to say to you, "Tell me about yourself," you would most likely tell me a bit of your "life story." You tell stories, literally, all the time. When you see a good friend or talk to a loved one, you usually tell him or her things through narratives. We express the joy of birth and cope with the great sorrow of death through narratives. Television shows, movies, songs, video games, and commercials are all presented in narrative forms. They aim to draw us into their worldview and hope, in some way, to affect us. Good narratives can make us feel certain emotions. Why would you cry over a death of a *fictional* character in a movie or a book? Narratives can also give us new insight to questions in life, as well as affirm and confirm feelings and insights we already have.

There are reasons why your family tells stories during the holidays, why your friends like to tell stories of your time together, why couples share the moments of when they met, why schools and institutions and communities often tell stories of their founders and important people. Narratives give meaning and direction to our lives. They help create a sense of identity and belonging. In this context, the importance of narratives is that they communicate moral ideas to us. Narratives influence our feelings toward moral issues, inviting us to think in particular ways about moral issues, and they give us grounding to be moral.

Moral theology begins with narratives, and it cannot exist without narratives. The primary source of narratives in moral theology is, of course, the Bible. The creation stories, the Exodus narrative, and so many other biblical stories provide foundational motifs for moral theology. Most importantly, the narrative of Jesus—his life, death, and resurrection, and particularly his teachings and actions—is crucial for moral theology (which is why you will see constant references to Jesus and biblical narratives in this book).

The significance of narrative for moral discourse opens up interesting questions. Consider this: I once overheard a person explaining a situation by telling a story. To put it a better way, she was retelling the events that occurred in a particular situation. As with many narratives, this retelling had a flow to it. It had a beginning, middle, and end. It also had a context and characters who did things and said things. The storyteller was speaking to two people. The intriguing point here is that the two people responded to the story differently; that is to say, they interpreted the story differently. A good story is open to multiple interpretations. This is particularly true of biblical stories.

I do not intend to give a full theory of biblical interpretation here, but I think we can note that there seem to be at least three distinctive ways that biblical stories invite themselves to be interpreted. The first and most basic interpretive method is to seek in a biblical story a takeaway point or points. In other words, there is a moral to the story. For example, one might say that the moral of the Prodigal Son (Luke 15:11-32) is that God's love for us, God's desire to be in union with us, is so strong that it overcomes our sins.

The second interpretive method invited by some biblical stories is to read them as analogies. Particular elements in a story stand for things outside the story. The parable of the Sower (Matt. 13:1-23) is presented in this form. Jesus tells the story of a person who is planting seeds. Not all the seeds are planted on good soil; some fall on the rocky ground. Jesus then explains that the seeds that fell on rocky ground are the people who joyously accept the word of God, but because their faith does not develop roots, it does not endure during trouble. The seed on good soil is the person who hears the word and understands it. This person, like a healthy plant, bears fruit.

When people attempt to apply biblical stories to their lives or their situations, they use analogy. Very often readers, for example, "see themselves" in a story. Perhaps the strongest analogical interpretation of Scripture we find is the way oppressed peoples throughout history have seen their story in the Exodus account. They recognize themselves as the contemporary slaves looking for God to hear their cries and to liberate them (Exod. 1–3).

The third interpretative method invited by a biblical text is to see the "point" of the story not so much as a moral idea as a feeling. Some biblical stories are, quite frankly, disconcerting and shocking. It is clear that some of Jesus' parables were meant to be provocative. He wanted to disturb his listeners.[1] When we hear the parable of the Good Samaritan, for example, we might embarrassingly recall times that we have passed by or ignored a person in need. We have all been priests and Levites. The point of the story, then, is not so much a moral one as it is to get us to think about who we are and why we are that way. It is a challenge for the heart as much as it is a message for the head.

If moral theology begins with narrative, it is appropriate to begin this book with a narrative. We start not with one meant to be provocative or one meant to be interpreted analogously. We begin with one that asks for a simple interpretation and invites a number of takeaway points. This story, or rather this collection of three stories, is perhaps the most informative story in the Bible for moral theology, because it offers a framework for understanding the subject and primary object of moral theology: the person. We open with the first three chapters of Genesis.

Beginning Moral Theology: Genesis 1–3

Genesis 1–11 is an ancient story of origins, often described as primeval history. Biblical scholars Richard Clifford and Roland Murphy write that we find here "an unusually sustained 'philosophical' and 'theological' explanation of the human race—its relation to God, its institutions, its flaws, its destiny—and of God and God's justice and abiding fidelity to the race."[2] Genesis 1–3, the creation stories and story of disobedience to God, ought then to be read as a text about "how things are" rather than as a text explaining "how things came to be." The text is an ancient yet profound narrative of enduring relevance for our understanding persons and being human. It is about meaning, not about science. When we read Genesis 1–3, we can learn a little bit about ourselves.

What follows here is a swift review of Genesis 1–3. The text itself is richer, more complex, and more poetic than this presentation (feel free to read the original yourself!). After the summary, we will reflect on the implications of the text for moral theology.

Genesis Chapter 1 narrates the well-known story of the creation of the cosmos in six days. On day one, God creates the light that he sees is good. On day two, we read that God separates the waters; some water goes under the dome and the rest above the dome. On day three, God again performs an action that "separates": this time, he separates the water from the dry land. This he also sees as good. God then has the earth put forth plants, fruit, and trees. Again, God sees this as good. On day four, God creates the lights in the dome of the sky. This provides light for earth. God sees this as good, too. On the fifth day, God has swarms of creatures come from the water, including birds that fly across the sky. God sees this as good and blesses the creatures. On day six, God creates animals, and again sees this as good. Then God creates humans and he gives them dominion over the creatures: "So God created humankind in his image, in the image of God he created them; male and female he created them" (Gen. 1:27). God blesses the woman and the man and tells them that he has given them the plants to eat. The text concludes, "And it was so. God saw everything that he had made, and indeed, it was very good" (1:30–31). The story ends (in Gen. 2:2) with the seventh day. God blesses the seventh day and rests from all his work.

Immediately following is another origins story. The story begins with God creating a man with dust from the ground. God gives the man life by breathing into his nostrils. Next God creates a garden and then, in a well-known passage, prohibits the man from eating from one of the trees. God says, "It is not good that man should be alone;

I will make him a helper as his partner" (2:18). God creates animals and birds and has the man name them, but none is found suitable as a helper. Next God puts the man to sleep and creates a woman out of one of his ribs. The man says, "This at last is bone from my bones and flesh of my flesh; this one shall be called Woman, for out of Man this one was taken" (2:23). The narrator comments, "Therefore a man leaves his father and his mother and clings to his wife, and they become one flesh. And the man and his wife were both naked, and were not ashamed" (2:24). Thus ends the second story.[3]

In Genesis 3:1, we are introduced to a new character, the serpent. The text describes him simply as "more crafty than any other animal that the Lord God has made" (3:1). The serpent talks to the woman and challenges God's prohibition to eat of the fruit of the tree. The woman sees the tree and realizes the benefits of eating its fruit. So she does. Her husband also eats the fruit.

After the man and the woman ate the fruit, their "eyes were opened" (3:7) and they come to the knowledge of their nakedness. They cover themselves and hide from God. God finds them and questions the man. He replies, "The woman whom you gave to be with me, she gave me fruit from the tree, and I ate" (3:13). God then asks the woman and she responds, "The serpent tricked me, and I ate" (3:13). God then curses the serpent. God tells the woman she will have pain in childbearing and that her husband will "rule over her" (3:16). To the man he says that the ground is cursed because of him and adds, "By the sweat of your face you shall eat bread until you return to the ground" (3:19). The man then names the woman "Eve" (we do not learn the man's name, Adam, until 4:25, after the Cain and Abel story). God makes clothes for the couple and expels them from the garden.

Implications for Moral Theology

The takeaway points of these stories for moral theology are enormous. Put simply:

1. All things are from God and are gifts from God.

2. Creation, everything, is good. Nonhuman creation is good regardless of its usefulness to persons.

3. Persons are in relation to God, other parts of creation, and other persons.

4. Persons have a distinctive position in creation. They are in the "image and likeness of God" and have "dominion" over creation.

5. Persons have the basic freedom and ability to deny or reject points 1 through 4.

Genesis 1–3 (as does Psalm 104, quoted at the beginning of this chapter) presents a cosmos dependent on the creative and sustaining activity of God. Moral theology recognizes this and is indeed a response to this. It notes that God creates all things and all things God creates are good. It also notes that not everything in creation is simply there for human consumption. There is a fundamental sense of dependence on God here, but this sense is invigorated by an equal sense of gratitude. Creation, life, is a gift.

Moral theology describes persons in their individual and relational senses. God created particular persons, distinct from each other but deeply related to each other. Persons exist in relation to God and to the whole of creation. The climax of both Genesis stories is the creation of persons in their basic relationship, their relation to each other. In the first story, the couple is created in the "image and likeness" of God and God gives them "dominion" over the creatures. This simple line has significant ramifications for moral theology.

One ramification of the "image of God" language is that it affirms the basic dignity of all persons. This phrase is the grounding idea in moral theology. All persons possess a sacredness. From this dignity and sacredness arise the basic moral claims and rights of persons that all must respect as a condition of human relationships. A second ramification of the "image of God" language is that it directs people to a particular way of living. Persons are created to be God's responsible representatives on earth.[4] The dominion God gives to the man and woman is to care for creation, including other people, as God would care for it. In relation to nonhuman creation, God sets up an arrangement like that between an owner and a manager.[5] In traditional language, persons are stewards of God's creation. As created in the image of God, persons are to reach out to, protect, nurture, care for, develop, share with, and give to others in the created world.

The foundation of moral theology, then, rests on these two key points: As God sees all persons in God's image, so must we; and as God gives, creates, and sustains, so must we. This story of grace and goodness is, however, not the whole story of Genesis 1–3. Humans are also like God in the sense that they are free. In this case, they were free to deny their nature. It is noteworthy that the woman makes a conscious choice to eat the fruit. She considered the goods involved, namely the taste of the fruit and the fact that eating it would make her wise. If she ate the fruit, she would be "like God," an offer hard to turn down! The woman acted not on impulse but on a rational, if misbegotten, choice. God did not interfere with her choice or the man's choice. Yet there is more.

After they eat the fruit, the man and woman hide. God finds them and questions them. What is their response? They both deny personal responsibility. The man says: "The woman whom you gave to be with me, she gave me the fruit from the tree, and I ate." In other words, he says it is God's fault that he ate the fruit! The woman in turn blames the serpent. Neither will admit of their choice. They acted freely and they freely rejected responsibility. Both choices illustrate the fundamental freedom persons have.

Humans are to be responsible agents in the world toward each other and toward nature. They also have the ability to think about themselves in these relationships and the power to make choices in line with their responsibilities. They have freedom and conscience. There would be no need for morality if we were not able to freely choose.

This section of the chapter has accomplished two things. It first described narrative as a form of moral discourse. It then looked at a narrative and unpacked the implications of that narrative for thinking about morality. Not all narratives, indeed not all biblical narratives, have the moral significance of Genesis 1–3, but nevertheless, many narratives are told to influence our sense of the right and the good. More importantly, narratives help form our sense of moral identity. We end this section with a quote from Leslie Marmon Siko's great novel *Ceremony*. This quote highlights the significance of narrative for our lives. "I will tell you something about stories, they aren't just for entertainment. Don't be fooled. They are all we have. . . . You don't have anything if you don't have stories."[6]

The Preacher: Prophetic Discourse

> Thus says the LORD. . . I will not revoke the punishment; because they sell the righteous for silver, and the needy for a pair of sandals—they who trample the head of the poor into the dust of the earth, and push the afflicted out of the way; father and son go in to the same girl, so that my holy name is profaned.

> Hear this word, you cows of Bashan who are on Mount Samaria, who oppress the poor, who crush the needy, who say to their husbands, "Bring something to drink!"

> They hate the one who reproves in the gate, and they abhor the one who speaks the truth. Therefore because you trample on the poor and take from them levies of grain, you have built houses of hewn stone, but you shall not live in them.

> Seek good and not evil, that you may live; and so the LORD, the God of hosts, will be with you, just as you have said. Hate evil and love good, and establish justice in the gate.

> Take away from me the noise of your songs; I will not listen to the melody of your harps. But let justice roll down like waters, and righteousness like an ever-flowing stream.
>
> —Amos 2:6–7, 4:1; 5:10–11, 14–15, 23–24

Preachers often tell stories in their sermons and homilies. But they often use other forms of moral discourse as well. One popular technique to get people's attention is to use hyperbole, purposeful exaggeration. I am sure that you have at one time or another used an exaggeration to get your point across. Other methods include the use of strong, passionate language and vivid images to capture the imagination of listeners. Still others simplify complex issues into either/or, or good/bad propositions. Perhaps the most popular form of "The

Preacher" can be seen on the back bumpers of cars. Bumper stickers often distill controversial issues into a few words, hoping to change the minds of people in the cars behind them.

Complementing his use of parables, Jesus used dramatic language. Indeed, there is a group of his teachings that is often referred to as the "hard sayings," because they make seemingly impossible demands. Jesus intended to provoke a response from his listeners. People, even those who generally take a literal reading of the Bible, know that their meanings lie beyond the literal. The most famous is perhaps from his Sermon on the Mount. Jesus said, "If your right eye causes you to sin, tear it out and throw it away; it is better for you to lose one of your members than for your whole body to be thrown into hell. And if your right hand causes you to sin, cut it off and throw it away; it is better for you to lose one of your members than for your whole body to go into hell" (Matt. 5:29–30). There is a deep moral challenge in his words here, but that challenge has nothing to do with self-mutilation. In the words of one recognized commentator, "The point is that Jesus calls for a radical ordering of priorities. The logic of one's decisions and moral choices is important. It is better to sacrifice a part of one's moral freedom than to lose the whole."[7]

In speaking this way, Jesus is following a long tradition. The prophets of the Old Testament often used hyperbole and passionate language to get the people to examine and then to change their behaviors. The series of quotations opening this section are from the book of Amos, one of the "major" prophets in the Old Testament. We see that he is an impassioned defender of justice and righteousness, and a strong critic of the powerful who "crush" the poor. Strong, passionate language can be very effective. It can also be alienating. No one, particularly those in power, wants to be criticized. Prophetic language aims to stop us in our tracks and force us think about our lives and our choices. The prophets want us to change. Put simply, prophets are like the conscience for the community.

Dr. Martin Luther King Jr. expertly and effectively used "The Preacher" model of moral discourse. There is no better example of this than his famous "I Have a Dream" address. The speech is packed with dramatic language, vivid images, and passionate verse. Note how King's moral claims are wrapped up in prophetic language.

The life of African Americans, he said, "is still sadly crippled by the manacles of segregation and the chains of discrimination. One hundred years later [after the Emancipation Proclamation], the Negro lives on a lonely island of poverty in the midst of a vast ocean of material prosperity. . . . But we refuse to believe that the bank of justice is bankrupt. We refuse to believe that there are insufficient funds in the great vaults of opportunity of this nation. And so, we've come to cash this check, a check that will give us upon demand the riches of freedom and the security of justice."[8]

King famously encourages his listeners not to turn back and not to despair in the face of these conditions. "Now is the time to rise from the dark and desolate valley of segregation to the sunlit path of racial justice. Now is the time to lift our nation from the quicksands of racial injustice to the solid rock of brotherhood. Now is the time to make justice a reality for all of God's children. . . . So I say to you, my friends, that even though we face the difficulties of today and tomorrow, I still have a dream. It is a dream deeply rooted in the American dream."[9]

Every American today is aware of his dream, including the often quoted line, "I have a dream my four little children will one day live in a nation where they will not be judged by the color of their skin but by the content of their character."[10] King concludes the speech by quoting the song "America" (*My Country 'tis of Thee*), and its famous refrain: "Let freedom ring." "And," he says, "when we allow freedom to ring, . . . we will be able to speed up that day when all God's children . . . will be able to join hands and to sing in the words of the old Negro spiritual, 'Free at last! Free at last! Thank God Almighty, we are free at last!' "[11] King's speech is still moving today. It continues to ask the question, "Which side are you on?" Prophetic language is fashioned to provoke a response in the listeners. Often the choice is put in either/or terms.

One of my favorite theologians is St. Augustine (d. 430). He is fun to read and study because his writings are full of passion and insight. He was a prolific writer, publishing over a hundred books along with two hundred letters and five hundred sermons. He tends to fit The Preacher model at times. For example, his most quoted moral advice, while very true, is perhaps too simple to base one's life on. He told people to, "Love and do what you will."[12] At times he distilled complex issues, as many preachers do, into a clear and direct choice:

> In this life there are two loves wrestling with each other in every trial and temptation: love of the world and love of God. And whichever of these two wins, that's where it pulls the lover as by the force of gravity. It isn't, you see, on wings or on foot that we come to God, but on the power of our desires. And again, it isn't with knots and chains that we find ourselves stuck to the earth, but with contrary desires. Christ came to change our love, and to make lovers of the heavenly life out of earthly lovers.[13]

There are many examples in the tradition of this kind of either/or moral call. Here are a few famous others. In Deuteronomy, God says, "See, I have set before you today life and prosperity, death and adversity.... Choose life so that you and your descendants may live" (Deut. 30:15, 19). Jesus likewise says, "Whoever is not with me is against me, and whoever does not gather with me scatters" (Luke 11:23). In the famous description of love in I John, the author writes, "Whoever does not love abides in death" (1 John 3:14). Finally, some contemporary moralists like to speak in this way about our cultural wars. We live today, they say, not in a "culture of life" but a "culture of death."

Moral theology lives in the contemporary context. It affirms, defends, and protects that which is good and right in ordinary life and it challenges all that is destructive to the good and right. It lives within both Genesis 1-2 and Genesis 3. Humans and creation are good. Humans, however, have the freedom and power to reject the good. The Preacher and prophetic discourse, then, are important elements in moral theology. They are meant to disturb us with bold appeals to clear right and wrong, good and evil. They want you to see how you participate and contribute to the good and to the evil. Prophets demand that you, in the words of Amos, "Seek good and not evil," indeed "Hate evil and love good," so that justice will "roll down like waters, and righteousness like an ever-flowing stream." But, you may ask, "What is the good?" "What is justice?" Prophetic discourse, like its three counterparts in moral discourse, is necessary for morality, but by itself, it is not enough. We need ethics.

The Voice of Reason: Ethical Discourse

Charity is the friendship of man for God.

Prudence is wisdom concerning human affairs.

Justice is a habit whereby a man renders to each one his due by a constant and perpetual will.

Fortitude may be taken to denote firmness only in bearing and withstanding those things wherein it is more difficult to be firm.

Temperance signifies moderation, which reason appoints to human operations and passions. . . . It withdraws man from things which seduce the appetite from obeying reason.

—Thomas Aquinas, *Summa Theologica,*
II–II, 23.1, 47.2, 58.1, 123.2, 141.2

There are no stories in the passages above. There is no passionate language. The author has no interest in catching your emotions. He does, however, want you to *think* a certain way. He wants you to understand certain key words in moral theology. What we see here is a third form of moral discourse, namely, ethics. If narrative and prophetic discourse tend to speak to your heart, ethics appeals to your head. Ethics plays a vital role in moral theology. Indeed for many people, ethical discourse is the fundamental voice in moral theology. There are two basic objectives of ethics. Ethics clarifies moral ideas by offering definitions and appropriate distinctions. Ethics also offers reasons, both conceptual and motivational, for morality. By conceptual reasons, we mean the justification for moral positions. Motivational reasons address the question of why one should be moral at all.

Ethics Clarifies Moral Issues

The paragraph opening this section contains five quotations from St. Thomas Aquinas (d. 1274), all of which define a particular virtue. Aquinas uses precise words to describe these moral terms as he begins his reflections on them. The point here is that we ought to start our thinking about moral issues with a common understanding. We cannot go very far in moral conversations if we are unclear about the meaning of moral ideas. Indeed, at the basis of some moral disagreements is a misunderstanding of the terms we are talking about. For example, it is hard to talk about racism when everybody in the room has a different definition of racism. A primary task of ethics is to define moral terms.

It is interesting to note that moral theology may define moral terms differently from other forms of ethics. That is to say, the Christian notion of love or justice, founded on biblical sources, may be different from a non-Christian definition of the same. And even Christians may understand the meaning of responsibility and answer the question, "Who is my neighbor?" in distinct ways.

Good moral judgment relies on clarity in thought, and it is the task of ethics to make relevant distinctions. Consider the following ethical reflection on end-of-life decisions: There is a difference between allowing a person to die from the causes of an incurable illness and mercy killing. Mercy killing is distinct from suicide, which itself is different from assisted suicide. Ethical discourse explains why these distinctions are important and argues that they are crucial in considering end-of-life decisions.

Consider another example. We all know the moral law, "Do not kill." But not all killing is the same. Directly and intentionally killing an innocent person is not the same as accidentally killing a person. Killing in self-defense is different from killing someone in an attack. Killing in war is different from killing in peace. Even in war, killing a civilian is different from killing a warrior. Ethical discourse labors to set these actions apart because, quite frankly, they are not the same actions. Defining moral terms and making relevant distinctions are essential elements of moral reasoning and thus a critical task of ethics.

Ethics Gives Reasons

Yet there is more to ethics than seeking clarity in our thinking about moral issues. The primary task of ethics is to give conceptual and motivational reasons. Let us consider conceptual reason-giving. This is very easy to understand. You do it all the time. For example, you think the intentional killing of an innocent person is wrong. Why? You probably also think that spreading nasty and untrue rumors about a person's sexual past is morally wrong. Why? You probably also think that breaking into another's apartment and taking someone's money and jewelry is morally wrong. Why? When you start to reflect on why you think these things are wrong, you are engaging ethical discourse. More importantly, when you tell me why these things are wrong, or when you try to influence my view of these actions, you are engaging in ethical discourse.

This is a very important aspect of moral theology. When you give reasons for your moral positions, you attempt to make your views intelligible and accessible to others.[14] Giving reasons, though it comes from your heart and your mind, is fundamentally external; its object is the heart and the mind of the other. This is not easy, because often our views are pre-rational. That is to say, they are informed by our intuitive thoughts. Think of this process as moving from the subjective experience of value to the objective realm of the shared experience of value.

When you give reasons you first must recognize some common ground with the person or group with whom you are talking (intelligibility). The successful process of giving reasons reaches out to the other through some commonality. You must in some way "speak the language" of the other. You try to "make sense" to the other (accessibility). Consider the words ethicists use to describe this process. You ground your position; you support your position; you back up your position; you justify your position; you give warrants for your position.

Generally speaking, we can distinguish two types of conceptual reason. The first type is aimed at persons in general; the second type is directed at persons as members of particular groups or with a specific identity. The first type is "public," as it recognizes a basic rationality among persons and appeals to the fundamental ability of persons to reason. This type of ethics assumes that you can engage in moral discourse with persons with whom you have little in common.

The other type of reason-giving is more restrictive. This type of reasoning appeals not so much to the common humanity of others as to something more specific the person shares with the other. Thus in presenting reasons for your moral positions, you appeal to some commonality. For sake of simplicity, let's call this "communal" reasoning. When Jews make moral arguments to Jews, they quote their sacred and traditional texts. When Muslims make moral arguments to Muslims, they quote the Qur'an, the sayings of the prophet Muhammad, and historic commentaries. When Christians make moral arguments to other Christians, they use the Bible to support their positions. Catholics might also use statements from councils and popes to convince other Catholics of moral positions. This sort of reason-giving is "in-house," as it appeals to the shared values of the persons as members of specific groups instead of the more public reason-giving.

A very interesting example of the use of the two types of moral reasoning is found in Dr. Martin Luther King Jr.'s famous 1963 "Letter from Birmingham Jail." The letter, literally written while King was in jail, was a response to a letter published in the Birmingham newspaper critical of King's work. Eight white clergymen from Birmingham (five bishops, two ministers, and a rabbi) wrote an open letter to the black community in Birmingham urging them to stop the civil rights demonstrations. The clergymen were particularly worried that outsiders (i.e., Dr. King) were leading these demonstrations. His participation in these demonstrations led to King's arrest.

In his letter of response, King addresses a number of topics, including the justification for his method of nonviolent direct action. He seeks common ground with these clergymen, supporting his views with reasons from the shared traditions of his audience. For Catholics, he cites the Bible, Augustine, and Aquinas. For Protestants he cites the Bible, Augustine, Luther, and John Bunyon. Indeed, as part of his letter, he even refers to the very prominent Jewish philosopher, Martin Buber. This, as well of his use of the prophets (and three other Old Testament figures), is an appeal to the rabbi.

King also offers a second type of communal-based reasoning. As he is writing to Americans (he notes that "Anyone who lives in the United States can never be considered an outsider anywhere in his country"[15]), he gives reasons based on the shared American moral and political traditions. He thus cites the Pilgrims, the Declaration of Independence, the First Amendment, Thomas Jefferson, Abraham Lincoln, and the 1954 Supreme Court decision outlawing segregation in public schools to justify his moral positions.

The most quoted section of the letter is his reflection on the morality of law and his description of unjust law. While Augustine and Aquinas introduce the topic for him, King ultimately appeals to the basic rationality and humanity of his audience. His reasoning here is independent of any specific group membership; that is to say, it is an example of public reasoning. He writes, "Any law that uplifts human personality is just. Any law that degrades human personality is unjust. All segregation statutes are unjust because segregation distorts the soul and damages the personality. It gives the segregator a false sense of superiority and the segregated a false sense of inferiority."[16] He continues,

> An unjust law is a code that a majority inflicts on a minority that is not binding on itself. This is difference made legal. . . . An unjust law is a code inflicted upon a minority which that minority had no part enacting or creating because they did not have the unhampered right to vote. . . . There are some instances when a law is just on its face and unjust in its application. For instance, I was arrested Friday on a charge of parading without a permit. Now there is nothing wrong with an ordinance which requires a permit for a parade, but when the ordinance is used to preserve segregation and to deny citizens the First Amendment privilege of peaceful assembly and peaceful protest, then it becomes unjust.[17]

In one writing, King presents both public and communal reasoning. Indeed, he has two sorts of communal reasoning. He appeals to the religious traditions of his critics and to the American narrative to which they all belong. In his discussion of morality and law, his reasoning is public. He appeals to the basic rational claims about the nature of justice and law, which he thinks all people of good will would understand.

Here is an important point: King's use of ethical discourse is characteristic of moral theology in general. First and foremost, moral theology appeals to the experience of the reality of God, known particularly through Jesus and mediated through tradition. It is then communal reasoning. At the same time, moral theology appeals to the basic humanity and reasoning of persons. Grounded on the stories of creation, as well as other biblical texts, moral theology appeals to human dignity and a fundamental sense that persons are, or can be, rational. The ethics of moral theology runs on two tracks, like a train. One rail of the track is Scripture (and the history of its interpretation), and the other is reflection on personhood (which includes the variety of sources of understanding what it means to be a person).

Yet backing up or grounding moral ideas is never enough for persons. When push comes to shove, people, all of us, need a basic reason to be moral in the first place. That is to say, why should we care? Ethics also addresses the "Why be moral at all?" question. People are moral for all sorts of reasons. Certainly fear of punishment for being immoral moves some people to act or not act. Others do the right thing because they hope for some reward or recognition or some other good to come from being moral. Morality is, after all, concerned with human flourishing, so arguments based on self-interest are not totally off base, though they seem to be immature at times. Why be moral? Many people are moved to do the right thing by their family or community or indeed for the human community. These reasons then go beyond self-interest, and are certainly laudable. Acting to promote the flourishing of others is central to morality. Some people, it is said, are motivated and inspired by universal principles.[18]

Moral theology affirms all these sorts of reasons but puts them in their proper place. Morality is, after all, a set of expectations aimed to enhance the flourishing of persons and their relationships, communities, and environments. But moral theology always points to something more: The moral life is, in the end, a response to God, now and here. "Thy Kingdom come, thy will be done, on earth," meaning today and at this moment. Distilled to the basics, we are not moral so we can get into heaven or avoid hell. We are moral because, from our heart, we know that our "being and doing" matter, in all our relationships, but primarily in our relationship to God. Being moral is not so much the path to eternal life as much as it is a present sense of being in relation to God. Reflecting on the whole of biblical morality, Scripture scholars remind us that "union of life with the Father in the kingdom of heaven is impossible without having lived in union with him in our earthly lives."[19]

Moral theology is a matter of the heart and the mind. Narrative and prophetic discourse appeal to our emotions and affections. We cannot discount the importance of our emotional life in our morality. Your sense of morality is deeply tied to who you are. You feel good when you do the right thing and you feel bad when you do not. Yet you know that you cannot simply act on feelings. You need to be thoughtful. There are some decisions that demand reflection and thinking. Ethics is a response to this need. Moral theology is a matter of the heart and the mind, but it is more than that. Moral theology is about doing things. It is about following up on feelings and conclusions. Thus we arrive at the fourth form of moral discourse: policy.

The Lawyer: Policy Discourse

University of St. Thomas (St. Paul, Minnesota)
Hate Crimes and Bias-Motivated Incidents Policy[20]

In determining whether alleged conduct is a hate crime or a bias-motivated incident, the university shall consider the record as a whole and the totality of circumstances, including the nature of the incident and the context in which the alleged incident(s) occurred. While related statements, practices and procedures are elaborated in other University documents (i.e., *Code of Conduct, Faculty Handbook, Employee Handbook, Statement on Offensive Behavior*), individuals determined to have violated this policy shall be sanctioned and subject to a range of disciplinary measures up to and including termination and expulsion.

As used in this Policy, the following terms are defined:

"Hate crime": At [this institution], a hate crime is defined as an actual criminal offense motivated in whole or in part by the offender's bias toward the complainant based on race, color, gender, sexual orientation, age, national origin, religion or physical or mental disability.

"Bias-motivated incident": At [this institution], a bias-motivated incident is defined as conduct, speech or act of intolerance motivated by another's actual or perceived race, color, gender, sexual orientation, age, national origin, religion or physical or mental disability.

A bias-motivated incident may or may not be criminal in nature. Sufficient objective facts must be presented to lead a reasonable and prudent person to conclude that the actions in question may be motivated by bias toward or against a targeted individual or group.

* * *

U.S. Department of State[21]

The Department of State is committed to providing a workplace that is free from sexual harassment. Sexual harassment in the workplace is against the law and will not be tolerated. When the Department determines that an allegation of sexual harassment is credible, it will take prompt and appropriate corrective action.

What Is Sexual Harassment?

Unwelcome sexual advances, requests for sexual favors, and other verbal or physical conduct of a sexual nature constitute sexual harassment when:

1. An employment decision affecting that individual is made because the individual submitted to or rejected the unwelcome conduct; or

2. The unwelcome conduct unreasonably interferes with an individual's work performance or creates an intimidating, hostile, or abusive work environment.

Certain behaviors, such as conditioning promotions, awards, training or other job benefits upon acceptance of unwelcome actions of a sexual nature, are always wrong.

* * *

*Constitution of the United States,
First Amendment*

Congress shall make no law respecting an establishment of religion, or prohibiting the free exercise thereof; or abridging the freedom of speech, or of the press; or the right of the people peaceably to assemble, and to petition the Government for a redress of grievances.

* * *

Legal scholar and moral theologian Cathleen Kaveny writes, "It seems as if every complicated moral issue sooner or later becomes a legal issue."[22] She is, of course, correct. Think about the many complicated moral issues that arise in contemporary public life: abortion, government-sponsored torture, the use of drones to kill enemies, physician-assisted suicide, global warming, pollution and resource depletion, gun violence, marriage between persons of the same sex, the casual destruction of embryos, insurance companies having access to your genetic information, pornography, pesticides and herbicides in your food, the raising of animals for food in factory-like conditions, poverty and the distribution of wealth, racism, sexism, religious freedom, drug use, and so on and so on. The top two paragraphs in this section show attempts to incorporate moral issues, namely hate-based crime and sexual harassment, into policy. This section considers the complex relationship between moral theology and encoding moral positions into policy.

Morality and Law

Put simply, there are two ways morally serious persons can respond to public moral issues. These ways reflect the two modes of ethical reasoning discussed above. One can do something within his or her particular small community, or one can do something within the larger communities in which we live. Consider the first option. A small community of like-minded persons can agree that they will not have abortions or own guns or serve in the military or participate in immoral beginning-of-life technologies or in immoral end-of-life procedures. They might also agree to grow their own food or to share their wealth so none are poor, or appropriately use nonrenewable resources. Morality in this sense is a set of expectations for members of a certain community to enhance their flourishing. Morality is "in house." Persons in this view are not called to change the world, but are called to witness to the world a higher morality. Perhaps when nonmembers of the community see how the community lives and treats others, the nonbelievers will be influenced to live better lives. The takeaway point of this view is that morality and law are separate entities. For the sake of discussion, let's call this Model 1. If Christian moral theology took this approach, its purpose would be to serve Christians (and only Christians).

The other approach, while recognizing Christians may indeed be required to live lives of high moral standards, rejects the view that they ought not directly influence the broader communities in which they live. Moral theology has a public face as well as a communal face. This second approach has two expressions. The first is the view that morality and law are fundamentally the same thing. If then something is immoral, it is illegal (or it ought to be illegal) and if something is illegal, it is immoral. The expectations of morality, at least the behavioral expectations, ought to be codified in public law. Let's call this Model 2. The second expression of this view is that morality and law are related but not equivalent. Morality ought to influence law but not all aspects of morality ought to be encoded in law. This is Model 3.

Think of morality and law as two circles. Model 1 sees the circles as distinct and separate. They exist side-by-side but do not touch or influence one another. Model 2 sees the circles together; one is fully over the other. It is hard to tell morality from law in this model. Model 3 sees the circles overlapping. Put simply, in this view, some morality ought to be contained in law and some morality ought not to be contained in law. In other words, some law is moral, some law might be immoral, and some law is amoral.

Which model is normative? The Christian tradition has experienced and continues to experience all three. Historically speaking, mainstream moral theology has advocated Model 3. Model 3 is also the most difficult to actualize. Model 1 and Model 2 are conceptually easy. Advocates of Model 3 must offer criteria or standards to help us determine what morality ought to be encoded in law and what morality ought not be encoded into law.

Thomas Aquinas was a proponent of Model 3, and his medieval discussion of law remains a very helpful tool. Aquinas describes law as an "ordinance of reason for the common good, made by one who has care of the community, and promulgated."[23] Key to his position is that there is a distinction between morality, what he calls natural law, and human law or positive law. Human or positive law is what we call public policy. He writes: "Every human law has just so much of the nature of law, as it is derived from the law of nature. But if in any point it deflects from the law of nature, it is no longer a law but a perversion of law."[24] If a human law does not reflect morality, it is no law at all. Thus, as we have seen, there remains the real possibility that some human laws may indeed be immoral.

But this addresses only half of our problem. There's another question: should all that the natural law dictates (morality) be put into public policy? Aquinas writes: "The general principles of the natural law cannot be applied to all men in the same way on account of the great variety of human affairs: and hence arises the diversity of positive laws among various people."[25] What he is saying here is that while morality is same for all, the level of legislation of morality depends on the context and the culture.

Later he explains this (note the ethical distinctions he makes): "The purpose of human law is to lead people to virtue, not suddenly, but gradually. Law ought not lay upon the multitude of imperfect people the burdens of those who are already virtuous, namely that they should abstain from all evil. Otherwise these imperfect ones, being unable to bear such precepts, would break out into yet greater evils."[26] The moral expectations of law are then limited for Aquinas.

There is more "realism" than "idealism" in Aquinas's moral theology. He continues: "Human law is framed for a number of human beings, the majority of whom are not perfect in virtue. Wherefore human laws do not forbid all vices, but only the more grievous vices, from which it is possible for the majority to abstain; and chiefly those that are to the hurt of others, without the prohibition of which human society could not be maintained: thus human law prohibits murder, theft and such like. . . . Laws imposed on people should also be in keeping with their condition."[27]

Aquinas offers the wisdom of Isidore of Seville (d. 636), a theologian who lived some eight centuries before him, to describe the characteristics of a good law: "Law shall be virtuous, just, possible to nature, according to the custom of the country, suitable to place and time, necessary, useful; clearly expressed, lest by its obscurity it lead to misunderstanding; framed for no private benefit, but for the common good."[28]

John Courtney Murray (d. 1967), the influential theologian of the mid-twentieth century, continued Aquinas's work. In his classic 1960 book *We Hold These Truths,* Murray offers thoughtful and detailed reflections on morality and law. Like Thomas, he recognizes that the relation between morality and law is complex. He calls public policy "the meeting place of the world of power and the world of morality."[29]

Murray writes, "The moral aspirations of law are minimal. . . . It enforces only what is minimally acceptable, and in this sense socially necessary. Beyond this, society must look to other institutions for the elevation and maintenance of its moral standards; that is, to the church, the home, the school, and the whole network of voluntary associations that concern themselves with public morality in one or another aspect."[30]

He continues, "Therefore the law, mindful of its nature, is required to be tolerant of many evils that morality condemns. A moral condemnation regards only the evil itself, in itself. A legal ban on an evil must consider what St. Thomas calls its own 'possibility.'" Murray then offers several questions to help conceptualize matters, including, "Will the ban be obeyed, at least by the generality? Is it enforceable against the disobedient? . . . Is the instrumentality of coercive law a good means for the eradication of this or that social vice?"[31]

More recently, the American Catholic bishops, in a reflection on particular social questions, noted: "We are aware that the movement from [moral] principle to policy is complex and difficult and that although moral values are essential in determining public policies, they do not dictate specific solutions. They must interact with empirical data, with historical, social, and political realities, and with competing demands on limited resources."[32]

What Is Going On? What Is Possible?

When we engage in policy discourse, we cannot ignore two fundamental questions: "What is going on?" and "What is possible?" As the bishops note, the "soundness" of policy decisions does not rest simply on moral principles. Good policy must be based on "accurate information" and valid assumptions about the nature of the problems addressed.[33] The point here is that when we advocate for particular laws based on morality, we need to temper our idealism with a bit of realism. We need to do the best we can, and that best is hardly ever perfect.

Theologian and legal scholar Cathleen Kaveny argues that we ought to return to Aquinas's use of Isidore's criteria of a just law to direct this conversation. Her argument is compelling, because Isidore's criteria still seem appropriate today.

Isidore begins by stating that law ought to be *virtuous*. Kaveny notes two distinct purposes of law here. Some laws, and some views of the totality of law, she argues, function like a police officer. The purpose of law is to stop crime and to punish offenders. For Isidore, Aquinas, Kaveny, and indeed for moral theology in general, law does have this function, but at its best, it also has a deeper function. In Kaveny's words, law is and should be a "moral teacher."[34] Law is not simply meant to control people. It can serve to develop people. In Aquinas's terms, it can gradually lead people to virtue.

Law must be *just*. Justice is giving to persons what is due, taking into consideration three things: equity, that is to say, the basic human dignity of the person; fairness, appropriate and morally justifiable distinctions between persons; and concern for the vulnerable. Above, we read Martin Luther King's critique of unjust laws, laws that violated the basics of justice.

Thomas, through Isidore, notes that a law must be *possible to nature*. In one of his speeches, King said that the law cannot make a person love, but it can stop a person from lynching.[35] His words display the limits of law. Laws, to be good laws, have to be enforceable. That is to say, the laws must place reasonable expectations on persons. They must be based on a sensible understanding of persons and the human condition. As Aquinas notes, laws ought to be made for the majority of persons, not merely for saints. Thus the requirement that a law must be *possible to nature*.

While basic moral truths may not differ from culture to culture, the level of legal enforceability of morality certainly does vary. A good law, says Isidore, must be in accord with the *custom of the country* and *suitable to place and time.* We have seen in history problematic attempts of missionaries and others who tried to regulate a form of morality that contrasted with deeply ingrained cultural practices. Certainly Prohibition laws in early twentieth-century America are an example of laws that contrasted with basic social customs.

Law must be *necessary.* It must address a real issue around which there is communal consensus. Isidore says the law must also be *useful.* It must accomplish something in relation to the object desired. Note also that useful is distinct from perfect. A law can be a good law, from a moral perspective, if it makes positive steps in response to a large social problem. A good law may not permanently solve an issue, but it does make a positive and creative response to an aspect of the problem. To do this, a law must be *clearly expressed.* It must be made public and able to be understood by those affected.

Finally, according to Isidore, law must be *directed to the common good,* that is to say, it must develop and promote the social conditions that allow persons to flourish. As such, the promoter of such laws must rely on arguments that reach beyond the private to the public. Arguments from moral principle alone are seldom effective and thus must be coupled with other sorts of arguments. While advocates of some laws may be propelled to act on moral grounds, often their success in moving the broader community lies in more publicly acceptable grounds of general self-interest.

Action

Let's return for a moment to the writings of Martin Luther King Jr. We mentioned his "I Have a Dream" speech as an example of prophetic discourse and his "Letter from Birmingham Jail" as an example of ethical discourse (we could also offer it as an example of narrative discourse). Both were from 1963. The most dramatic event in the 1963 civil rights campaign was, however, not King's arrest or his letter from the jail or his famous speech on the Lincoln Memorial. For weeks after his arrest, the demonstrations continued in Birmingham, as thousands of young people marched in the streets. With television cameras rolling, the head of the city's safety department, Bull Connor, attacked a group of teenagers with police dogs and fire hoses. The attacks on these nonviolent demonstrators shocked the nation.[36] David Oppenheimer comments, "Outside the South, the media depictions of the attacks on the children had a dramatic effect on white public opinion. A few days earlier *Time* magazine and the *New York Times* were criticizing Dr. King as an unwelcome outsider in Birmingham; now they were editorializing against the police violence."[37]

Things changed: New laws were enacted in Birmingham and across the country. In Birmingham, changing rooms, rest rooms, drinking foundations, and lunch counters were desegregated by law. In 1964, President Johnson signed the Civil Rights Act, which prohibited discrimination based on race, color, religion, or national origin in places open to the public, in public education and the use of public finds, and in employment. In 1965, Johnson passed the Voting Rights Act. This law, among other things, made it illegal for states or local governments to legislate barriers to vote, such as literacy tests, based on race or social status. In 1968, a week after King's death, Johnson signed the Fair Housing Act, creating equal housing opportunities for persons regardless of race or social status.[38]

Dr. King's efforts, as highlighted in the "I Have a Dream" speech and his "Letter from Birmingham Jail," were aimed at conversion and transformation. In a legally segregated society, he believed integration would come from changing people's hearts and through legislation. His work has had an enduring effect on the nation.

His work also illustrates the four forms of moral discourse and suggests their relatedness. Responses to moral issues often begin with narratives, people telling their stories. But that is not enough for them to be heard by the larger community and indeed by those who hold power in such communities. Often it takes the prophet, people engaging in prophetic discourse, to critique the system and to call for change. At this point, members of the community are forced to think through the challenge and perhaps change the policy and social customs.

What This Means for Moral Theology

Moral theology needs all four forms of moral discourse, but recognizes that persons are called more to one or the other. It recognizes the limits of each and the interdependence of each. Moral theology also recognizes several other points from the discussion above. First, it notes that moral reflection is dependent on context. Dr. King's world and the narratives that informed his work is very different from the world I live in and the world you grew up in. King was able to bring moral theology to bear on a particular social environment. We are called to do the same, but our concerns, our driving themes, may be very different from his. Moral theology does not simply fall from the sky into our lives. It must be worked at to meet lives of real people.

While recognizing context, we must also realize our connectedness as persons. If nothing else, the Genesis stories illustrate our relatedness to God, to others, and to the rest of creation. With this relatedness comes responsibility, moral expectations about behavior and character. The four forms of moral discourse all aim to influence our conscience. They are used to influence our character, our sense of who we are as moral persons, as well as our particular behaviors. These themes will engage our attention in the chapters to come.

Moral Identity and Moral Authority

Three issues related to moral identity were addressed in this chapter. A key to your moral identity is finding your moral voice, that is to say, the form of moral discourse you are most comfortable with. Put simply, are you a storyteller, a person passionate about causes, a person who needs strong reasons for moral views, or one who prefers to do things rather than talk about things? Most of us tend toward one or the other. As you probably guessed by my interest in writing this book, I tend toward ethical discourse. How about you? Finding one's moral identity includes understanding one's moral voice.

Even though we tend toward one or the other, all four forms have had an impact on us. Indeed, at one time or another, we should be engaged in all of them. Everyone must recognize the significance of narrative in his or her moral formation. Stories literally surround us and influence us all the time. Everyone at some time in his or her life should be an Amos and, with a bit of passion, call people to "seek good" and to "establish justice." Everyone ought to be able to give reasons for their moral positions, that is to say, to move from subjective experience of value to an objective public meaning. Finally, we must figure out how we want to relate our moral views to the various communities in which we live, that is to say, our friendships, families, workplaces, neighborhoods, local communities, states, countries, and even on an international basis. Are you a Model 1, a Model 2, or a Model 3? A key element here is your ability to engage in other forms of moral discourse than the one you are most at home with. Do you have the ability to move out of your comfort zone to address an issue in a particular situation?

The second and third issues central to moral identity are introduced by the Genesis story in this chapter. The second concerns your personal appropriation of the "image of God" theme. Here is the basic question moral theology asks about your sense of moral identity: Do you think that you are an image of God? Seriously, do you think you have a basic dignity and a basic value (that you ought to respect and nurture and that others ought to respect and nurture)? The next question is related: Do you think others, even those who appear different from you, are in the image of God? Think about this.

The third issue central to moral identity, also introduced by the Genesis story, is your sense of persons in relation to creation. There seem to be four moral schemas for "seeing oneself" in nature.[39] The first is that persons are fundamentally consumers of the goods of the earth. The things of the earth, water, minerals, air, soil, animals, plants, exist for our use. The second is that persons are stewards or managers of the earth. The earth is for humans, but humans have a responsibility to tend it and care for it and to reasonably sustain it for future generations. The third is that persons are responsible members of the biotic community. Note the difference in the third from the second in its description of persons. While the person is distinct from nature in the second, the third sees persons as part of a web of interdependence. It sees human flourishing critically related to the flourishing of elements in nature. The fourth is that persons are egalitarian members of the biotic community. Persons with this view have very strong moral views on the use of animals and other elements in creation.

Your moral identity is linked to one of these four views. Does nature exist simply for human use? Do you have some responsibility to care for creation? Do you see yourself linked to things in nature and do you have a sense for the intrinsic worth of creation? Do you think that animals and perhaps other members of creation have strong moral claims, rights, like humans do? Given the view of persons in Genesis 1–2 as God's responsible representatives on earth, it seems that the second and third views are more congenial to moral theology. After reading Genesis, it would be hard to defend the view that the earth and things of the earth exist simply to fulfill human wants. It would also be hard to defend the view that all creatures on earth have a similar moral status. Persons have particular moral expectations to care for and cultivate the earth.

A related question to moral identity is moral authority. Your moral identity is related to your sense of moral authority. Who or what are moral authorities for you? There are at least three categories of people who have moral authority for you.

First, some people have moral authority for you based on the office or the recognized role they play in your life. We tend to think that public authorities (whether they be in religion, education, government, the military, or business) have moral authority for us because of their social position.

Second, at times you defer giving persons moral authority until you hear the substance of their moral discourse. You listen to a person's position, opinions, and so on, and then decide if it is authoritative for you. The storyteller's narrative has authority for you in relation to its power to engage you and to illuminate or to bring to light a pressing issue. The authority of the prophet's particular denunciation for you rests on the truthfulness of the critique, for example, of a cultural practice, in relation to a recognized standard, for example, the Gospel. The authority of the Voice of Reason rests on a set of "rules for arguing," for example consistency and coherence, but also on the sources that the person sites to justify the position. The authority of the lawyer or practitioner depends on their experience doing what they do.

The third source of moral authority is your sense of a person's moral identity. If a person seems to have a strong moral identity, put simply, if you think the person is a good person, we tend to grant them authority. Their moral identity influences our moral identity. Moral authority is then grounded on position, reason, and goodness. In the ideal situation the three converge. When conflict occurs, reason prevails over position. There is no stronger authority, however, than goodness.

Moral identity, then, is a very personal issue with significant social ramifications. You should cultivate it for its own good and for your own flourishing as a person. You should also cultivate it if you think that any time in your life you would want to be taken seriously as a moral person.

Questions

1. Briefly discuss the strengths and weaknesses of each of the four forms of moral discourse.

2. Evaluate one of the forms of moral discourse. What are its characteristics? Why do people tend to use it? What sort of responses are people looking for when they use it? What are the strengths and weaknesses of this form of discourse? Give a concrete example of this form of discourse.

3. Discuss how and why the author uses the Bible in this chapter (note the sources the author relies on). What might be different or alternative ways of using the Bible in this context? What is your response to the use of the Bible in this chapter?

CHAPTER TWO

Freedom and Expectations

The caged bird sings
with a fearful trill
of things unknown
but longed for still
and his tune is heard
on the distant hill
for the caged bird
sings of freedom.

Maya Angelou,
"Caged Bird"[1]

For you were called to freedom, brothers and sisters; only do not use
your freedom as an opportunity for self-indulgence, but through
love become slaves to one another. —St. Paul (Galatians 5:13)

As the Father has loved me, so I have loved you; abide in my
love. . . . This is my commandment, that you love one another as I
have loved you. No one has greater love than this, to lay down one's
life for one's friends. —Jesus (John 15:9, 12–13)

The opening quotation is the last stanza of Maya Angelou's
poem "Caged Bird." In the first stanza, Angelou beautifully describes
the habits of the free bird. It leaps on the wind and dips its wings and
claims the sky. The second and third stanzas of the poem describe
the caged bird, with its feet tied and wings clipped, singing out from
behind the bars of the cage for freedom. Its song for freedom is heard
in the distance on a far hill.

The fourth and fifth stanzas stand in contrast, as the free bird
expresses itself in its liberty while the caged bird in its "grave of
dreams" lives a nightmare. The final verse, quoted above, is a tribute
to the power of the human spirit even in times of oppression. The
caged bird, while having no physical freedom, freely and naturally
desires things beyond its experience. The bird movingly calls out for

what ought to be its own. It refuses to be restrained by the context and does not allow itself to be defined by the one who has clipped its wings and tied its feet. The poem is a tribute to the natural human desire for freedom and a condemnation of the oppression of that freedom.

The second and third quotations address a basic truth of moral theology. We are free and indeed we are to realize our freedom (and indeed help others to become "free birds"). Yet we are commanded to love. Love of God, love of neighbor, love of enemy, and love of self are central themes of the New Testament. A moral theology that does not prioritize the requirement of love is no moral theology at all. Together, the quotes display the fundamental issues of moral theology: we are free, yet there are expectations.

This chapter has two sections. The first section addresses freedom, and argues that persons experience freedom in four distinct but related ways. The second part of the chapter notes that morality is fundamentally about expectations about behavior and character in relation to the experiences of freedom.

The Four Senses of Freedom

Freedom is an essential characteristic of your functioning as a person. Think about this for a moment. What would life be like without freedom? It would certainly not be a life that you would want to live! The term freedom, however, has several meanings. Angelou's caged bird, with its clipped wings and bound feet living in a prison, has no freedom. At the same time, the bird freely sings a song so powerfully that it is heard on the distant hill. So what, then, do we mean by freedom?

Generally speaking, people experience freedom in four ways. In an effort to conceptualize this, think of a triangle[2] (I know a triangle has three parts!). The triangle I want you to imagine has a solid base and two sides about the same size. The triangle also has an "area," that is, the space inside the three lines—four parts in all.

We begin with a reflection on the base of the triangle, which we can call freedom from external interference. This first type of freedom refers to the way the word is frequently used. Freedom usually means being left alone or not being controlled by others. We then move to the two sides of the triangle. The one we can call freedom for simple goods and the other freedom for complex goods. These types of freedom are seen when people act to achieve goods and goals. They are personal, or are expressions of the personal. The fourth element of the triangle is the interior. Here we have fundamental freedom. This type of freedom, metaphorically called the "freedom of the heart," is the freedom from which persons make life commitments. It is the freedom where one accepts and experiences faith, hope, and love. The freedom here is to be a certain type of person.

Persons experience the first type of freedom passively; that is to say, we experience this when people leave us alone. The other types of freedom are experienced actively; that is to say, we experience the internal power to act in certain ways. Thus we can say that the first type of freedom is "external" and the latter three are "internal."

Freedom from External Interference

If you were asked the question, "When do you feel most free?" You would probably say something like, "When people leave me alone." Or, "When I am on vacation, and there is no one telling me what to do." New college students living away from home for the first time have intense experiences of this sense of freedom (and find it hard to go home for the holidays when this freedom is restricted). The first and most obvious experience of freedom is then *freedom from external interference.*

When most of us speak of freedom it is this basic experience we are referring to. Think of the many freedoms, or liberties, we have. When we say we live in a "free" country, we mean that we are free to say and write as we wish. We can freely elect our public officials. The corollary to this is that government must not interfere with our freedom to say or write what we want. We have the right to freedom of speech and right to freedom of the press. When people talk about the "free" market, they are referring to freedom in this sense. In the free market, people are free to buy, to produce, and to sell goods and commodities without (undue) government restrictions.

In contrast to some countries in the world, we have religious freedom. The government cannot regulate religion or individual religious choice. You are free to choose your religion and to practice it. You are also free not to choose a religion.

This first sense of freedom is rightly called *liberty* and its primary description is freedom from the interference of others. Patrick Henry's famous line in a 1775 speech captures the power of this type of freedom: "Give me liberty or give me death!" The founding documents of the United States, the Declaration of Independence and the Constitution, guarantee this sort of freedom. We experience it every day.

Interference in our activities or limitations on our actions can come from sources besides governments. Many people experience economic and social structures that force them into situations that they themselves would not choose to be in. Terrible working conditions and poverty, not to mention prejudices, racism and sexism, along with oppressive governments can and do limit people's freedom. All of this is to say that poverty, racism, and unjust economic and educational conditions, by definition, interfere with people's lives and thus their freedom.

Gaudium et Spes insightfully notes: "Now a man can scarcely arrive at the needed sense of responsibility, unless his living conditions allow him to become conscious of his dignity, and to rise to his destiny by spending himself for God and for others. But human freedom is often crippled when a man encounters extreme poverty just as it withers when he indulges in too many of life's comforts and imprisons himself in a kind of splendid isolation."[3]

But it is not just large impersonal forces that limit a person's basic freedom. We all know people who are "controlled" by their relationships. We all know people in "unhealthy" relationships, where they are limited and their development as persons is interfered with.

There is a very important moral point to this type of freedom. Freedom from external interference has a moral purpose. It provides the conditions for the possibility for us to flourish, to grow, and to develop as persons. The experience of external freedom sets the conditions for the experience of internal freedoms. Freedom from external interference allows persons to become "authors" of their lives.[4] It allows persons to take responsibility for their lives, to experience a sense of autonomy and indeed to be accountable for their actions. Oppression (the domination of one over another) and repression (violent or forced suppression of one over another) in political, economic, or social situations, or in interpersonal relationships violate a fundamental element of personhood and are thus morally wrong. Angelou's "Caged Bird" poem graphically illustrates this objective moral truth.

Freedom for Simple Goods and Freedom for Complex Goods

There is more to freedom than being *free from* the external control of others. We are also *free for* certain things. There are two experiences of freedom here. The first is your ability to direct your actions in simple and basic ways. You make simple choices to direct your actions all the time. You decided to read this. You decided to sit down when you started reading this. You decided where you would sit and how you would place your legs. Perhaps you decided to get something to eat or drink. Did you decide to turn on music while you read? What did you decide to eat today? Sometimes these choices have moral import and sometimes they do not. For simplicity, let's call this *freedom for simple goods*. You are able to direct your actions as you see fit.

The second type of *freedom for* is your ability to choose complicated life directions. You have the power to choose goals and purposes in life. You choose to do your homework (along with going to class, etc.) today because you are choosing to get a college degree, because two years from now, you want to get a job and maybe get married or perhaps buy a house down the line. You choose to run or lift weights in the gym (along with eating well) because you choose to be a healthy and strong person. We have the freedom not only to direct particular actions, like your reading this (a simple good), and we have the freedom to choose larger goals and purposes in our lives. Let's call this more multi-faceted and complicated coordination of actions and choices *freedom for complex goods*.

I assume that your pet dog has some limited level of freedom in the first sense (others may say that it is all instinct—that is to say, they believe dogs act without freedom). On the other hand, I know that your dog does not have the freedom to conceive and work through plans for what we are calling complex goods. Your dog is not planning for retirement.

The outside of the triangle is now complete. We have the base and two sides. An essential part of your experience of personhood is that you can choose goods in your life and you can choose to act to achieve those goods.

Freedom of the Heart

The base of the triangle refers to external factors controlling or not controlling your behavior. The sides of the triangle refer to your power to choose actions leading toward simple goods and complex goods. Yet there is a deeper type of freedom you experience; perhaps not often, but you experience it nevertheless. There are several words people use to describe this type of freedom: interior freedom, existential freedom, spiritual freedom, fundamental freedom, or freedom of the heart. All these words point to the sense that this type of freedom underlies or is basic to your sense of yourself and thus to your choices. It is here where the questions of moral identity get worked out.

This type of freedom has very little to do with constraints from outside. More often than not, it has to do with constraints on the inside. This freedom is not really about particular actions you might take, although actions would certainly come as a result. This type of freedom is related to the freedom to choose larger goals and directions in life, but it is not really the same thing. This type of freedom refers to your power to "do" something that precedes your ability to act. This type of freedom, so fundamental to the moral life, allows you to be you. The traditional word used to capture this freedom is the heart. "The heart is the place of decision, deeper than our psychic drives. It is the place of truth."[5]

For theologians, one's basic choices in the spiritual life are the most significant choices one can make. John Mahoney writes, for example, that underlying a person's "moral decisions for action is the basic disposition, or fundamental option" made by the person "towards objective good, or God."[6] Charles Curran writes, "At the core of her being, the individual makes this choice of God. The basic yes and commitment to God . . . become the fundamental option . . . and has a significant effect on the categorical choices that we make."[7]

Most people do not seem to make one "fundamental" choice in their lives. By the time we move into adulthood, most of us have made a handful of fundamental choices, fundamental commitments, to others and to ourselves, that direct our lives. This part of freedom, so important in the consideration of morality, is rarely talked about. Let's consider it from several examples.

In her book *Personal Commitments*, theologian Margaret Farley describes the nature of committed love. In an interesting section of the book she considers the significance of sacrifice in a relationship. After noting the importance of sacrifice, she reflects on whether all sacrifice is morally appropriate. In other words, she wonders if morality imposes limits on self-sacrifice. She concludes that we have "a moral obligation not to relate to another person in a way that is truly destructive of ourselves as persons." We may indeed have "to sacrifice our own welfare—sacrifice even our home, our health, our security, our reputation, our professional future, our very life."[8] That is to say, "while we may sacrifice everything we *have*, we may not sacrifice everything we *are*. We may not sacrifice in a final sense our autonomy. We may not sacrifice our capability for union and communion with God and human persons."[9] This "sense of our autonomy" is the freedom within the triangle. This freedom is an *essential element* of our personhood. It is wrong for us to give this up to anyone and it is wrong for anyone to expect us to give this up.

One way many of us experience this freedom is in moments of forgiveness. When someone hurts you, you may feel a sense of resentment. Most of us would say that this is a normal response. You were hurt. This resentment may linger in you. It could eat away at you and be a persistent feeling that comes, in a way, to control you. When you forgive someone, you choose to give up the resentment and not let these feelings control you.[10] When you forgive, you make an internal act of letting those feelings go. The act is wholly and fully yours. No one can make you forgive anyone. You do this from your own power. You are able to forgive because you have this interior freedom.

It is the same type of freedom that enables you to have faith. A critical doctrine of faith is that a person's "response to God in faith must be free: no one therefore is to be forced to embrace the Christian faith against his own will. . . . The act of faith is of its very nature a free act."[11] It is from deep within that we make faith commitments.

One of the reasons we take marriage so seriously is the act of consenting to marry, that is to say, the vows promised are thought by all to be made from one's fundamental freedom. If the priest or minister or judge does not believe that each person is acting in full freedom, he or she ought not preside over the wedding. The people marrying must be free from external restraint (no "shotgun" weddings) and they must be internally free to choose to marry the other. If they say the vows but do so with their freedom impaired, either internally or externally, there is no marriage. As theologian Michael Lawler commented, "For a valid marriage . . . only one moment of the ritual counts, the solemn moment of giving consent. . . . If that moment of free consent is missing or in any way flawed, there is no wedding and there is no marriage."[12]

A final illustration of this interior freedom comes from some of the most gripping literature I have read, namely the testimony of persons who survived Nazi concentration camps. Victor Frankl's *Man's Search for Meaning* immediately comes to mind. In that moving book, Frankl describes the absolute horrors of living and trying to survive in the camp. The book, however, is not simply about the evil of the Nazis. It is rather a testimony to fundamental freedom. After pages and pages describing the terrible conditions of the camp, Frankl writes about the people who were "able to retreat from their terrible surroundings to a life of inner riches and spiritual freedom."[13] He continues:

> Man *can* preserve a vestige of spiritual freedom, of independence of mind, even in such terrible conditions of psychic

and physical stress. . . . We who lived in concentration camps can remember the men who walked through the huts comforting others, giving away their last piece of bread. They may have been few in number, but they offer sufficient proof that everything can be taken from a man but one thing: the last of the human freedoms—to choose one's attitude in any given set of circumstances, to choose one's own way.[14]

These examples and illustrations suggest the importance of what we are calling "interior" freedom. This freedom is fundamental to personhood and thus to the moral life. We experience this freedom in our "heart."

The Situation of Freedom

Our freedoms are always limited by real life. We all face physical and psychological barriers. I am not "free" to jump over a building or lift 300 pounds. I cannot feed all the hungry kids in the world. I cannot cure cancer. I cannot perform brain surgery. My personal characteristics prohibit (or at least inhibit) my ability to act in certain ways, even though I might want to act in these ways. Lack of knowledge restricts my choices and my ability to act.

Addictions, by definition, restrict our freedom. Consider the following commentary on freedom from the National Institute on Drug Abuse:

> The initial decision to take drugs is mostly voluntary. However, when drug abuse takes over, a person's ability to exert self-control can become seriously impaired. Brain imaging studies from drug-addicted individuals show physical changes in areas of the brain that are critical to judgment, decision making, learning and memory, and behavior control. Scientists believe that these changes alter the way the brain works, and may help explain the compulsive and destructive behaviors of addiction.[15]

Diseases can also limit freedom and indeed can, in some instances, direct one's actions.

It is a long-held notion in Christian theology that sinfulness can limit people's freedom. We can live "under the slavery of sin" and not really be free to act as we want or we know we should. Consider two famous examples in Christian literature.

St. Paul in his Letter to the Romans captures, perhaps more dramatically than most of us might, makes an important point about this freedom. Sometimes we do things we know we should not do. Paul writes, "I do not understand my own actions. For I do not do what I want, but I do the very thing I hate. . . . I can will what is right, but I cannot do it. For I do not do the good I want, but the evil I do not want is what I do" (Rom. 7:15, 18–19). What Paul is saying is that in a very real way, he is not "free" to do the right thing. He is weakened by sin.

St. Augustine, in what is perhaps the most famous prayer in Christian autobiography, has a similarly striking line. As he is reflecting on his life as a young man, he writes that he was torn apart by his strong desire to seek God and his stronger desire to continue on with his life that was often driven by lust. Thus in brutally honest words, he asks God to give him "chastity and continence, but not yet."[16]

Both St. Paul and St. Augustine seemed to have made fundamental choices toward God in their hearts, yet they found themselves unable to do the right thing. There was some interior interference with their power to choose particular actions and to direct their lives to particular goals. But this interference came not from some economic or political power, but from their internal impulses. Their sin limited their freedom to act.

There is some irony here. Every person whom you would regard as being good and morally strong has made free choices to give up liberty over large portions of his or her life. In some ways, the morally mature person is less free than other people. If standards or expectations about conduct and attitudes are a central concern of morality, the moral person must necessarily follow these standards. To follow a standard is to submit oneself to an external authority. To be moral one must, to a certain degree, willingly surrender one's freedom in some ways. Yet to say that a morally mature person is one who merely submits to moral standards misses the deeper sense of morality.

Persons whom we tend to regard as morally strong and admirable are "free" from intentions and values that are trite or harmful. The people we highlight as morally strong are internally free from being dominated by the distractions of life. This enables them to see what really matters in life. Through this process, one's freedom of the heart can become more mature.

All morally mature people give up some of their freedom in the hopes of gaining more complex goals. When you get married, indeed when you are involved in a dating relationship, you, by the very nature of your commitment, willingly and happily choose to limit your liberty. When you get a job, buy that nice car, and get a mortgage, you are "tied down" in ways that your single, unemployed friends living with mom and dad are not. Wait until you have children! A part of being a morally mature person is to make life choices that in some ways limit your freedom (for both simple and complex goods) so you can attain greater fulfillment and flourishing, so as to seek particular higher complex goods. True and good choices here flow from of one's internal freedom.

The picture of freedom in this chapter rejects the idea that we are unable to choose actions and goals. That is to say, it rejects deterministic views of human nature. We do have these freedoms. We can work to create our moral identity. It also suggests that we are not purely and totally free. There are all sorts of internal and external things that constrict our freedom (again, these may indeed be chosen). *Our freedom is a situated freedom,* situated within a realistic view of the specific contexts of one's life. Our image of a triangle to represent freedom needs then to be surrounded by a circle. Our freedom is always within real life.

The Four Elements of Morality

Freedom, broadly understood to include the four senses of freedom discussed above, is the central and crucial experience of being a person. Because of this, we ought to respect our freedom and the freedom of others. Note the shift in language from the first sentence to the second sentence. The first was *descriptive*. A descriptive statement contains some fact or something that exists: we have freedom.

The second sentence is *normative*. A normative statement addresses something we ought to do. Note also that the normative flows from the descriptive. Morality, generally understood, contains both descriptive and normative elements; however, it is the normative that is primary. Simply speaking, we define morality in normative terms. Morality is a set of expectations about behavior and character for persons. We can describe these expectations in relation to our experiences of freedom. This next section considers the four basic elements of morality: rights, rules, intentions/goals, and habits. These four elements too can be described using the image of a triangle with three sides and an interior space.

Morality and Freedom from Interference: Human Rights

The very ground of moral thinking, the "base" of the triangle of the elements of morality, is a direct response to our fundamental sense of freedom. In order to act, we must be free. The essential sense of personhood is experiencing freedom from the interference of others. The "others" are persons, groups, institutions, governments, and "systems" created by persons. Yet we know that all too often in history, people are not free to act. The "Caged Bird" represents whole groups of persons in the past and in the present.

The "Caged Bird" needs freedom to fulfill its basic nature, but it needs more. It needs certain conditions to flourish, many of which are dependent on others. One might say that morality has arisen in human life because of a contradiction: we know freedom and basic human conditions are essential to our flourishing, yet we also know that too often persons dominate other persons. The base of moral expectations, the moral minimum, we might say, is that all persons have a set of fundamental claims to some simple goods. We call these "moral minimums" human rights.

Human rights are morally legitimate claims that all persons have because they are human. People are more likely to agree on the idea that such claims exist than to agree on a list of such rights. In the Catholic moral tradition, Pope John XXIII declared the classic list of human rights in his 1963 encyclical (an encyclical is a formal statement of Church doctrine by a pope) *Pacem in Terris*. Because, he says, persons have intelligence and free will they have the following rights:

The Right to a Life with Dignity: Every person has the right to life. Every person has the right to bodily integrity and to the means necessary for the proper development of life, namely food, clothing, shelter, medical care, rest, and, finally, the necessary social services. In consequence, every person has the right to be looked after in the event of ill health; disability stemming from his work; widowhood; old age; enforced unemployment; or when deprived of the means of livelihood.

Rights Pertaining to Moral and Cultural Values: Every person has the right to be respected. Every person has a right to a good name. Every person has a right to freedom in investigating the truth, and—within the limits of the moral order and the common good—to freedom of speech and publication, and to freedom to pursue whatever profession he or she may choose. Every person has the right, also, to be accurately informed about public events. Every person has the natural right to share in the benefits of culture, and hence to receive a good general education, and a technical or professional training consistent with the degree of educational development in one's own country.

The Right to Worship God according to One's Conscience: Every person has the right to worship God according to the dictates of individual conscience, and to profess faith both privately and publicly.

The Right to Choose Freely One's State in Life: Every person has the right to choose the kind of life that appeals to him or her. Every person has the right to found a family, where men and women enjoy equal rights and duties, or to embrace the priesthood or the religious life. The family, founded upon marriage freely contracted, one and indissoluble, must be regarded as the natural, primary cell of human society. The interests of the family, therefore, must be taken seriously into consideration in social and economic affairs, as well as in faith and morals. Each of these spheres has an impact on the strength of family and its ability to fulfill its mission. Parents have the primary right to support and educate their children.

Economic Rights: Every person has the inherent right to be given the opportunity to work, and to be allowed the exercise of personal initiative in work. Working conditions must not harm physical health, the morals of workers, or impair the normal development of young people. Women must be accorded such conditions of work as are consistent with their needs and responsibilities as wives and mothers. Each worker is entitled to a just wage. This must be especially emphasized. The amount a worker receives must be sufficient, in proportion to available funds, to allow the family a standard of living consistent with human dignity. Every person has the right to the private ownership of property, including that of productive goods. With this right comes a social obligation.

The Right of Meeting and Association: Humans are social by nature. Consequently all persons have the right to meet and to form associations. They have the right to organize associations as they see fit. They have also the right to exercise their own initiative and act on their own responsibility within these associations.

The Right to Emigrate and Immigrate: Every human being has the right to freedom of movement and of residence within the confines of one's own country. When there are just reasons in favor of it, every person must be permitted to immigrate to other countries and take up residence there. The fact that people are citizens of a particular country does not deprive them of membership in the human family, the global community.

Political Rights: Every person has the right to take an active part in public life, and to make a personal contribution to the common good. Every person is entitled to the legal protection of his or her rights. Such protection must be effective, unbiased, and strictly just.[17]

Pope John described these rights as universal, inviolable, and inalienable. "*Universal* because they are present in all human beings, without exception of time, place, or subject. *Inviolable* as they are inherent in the human person and in human dignity and because it would be vain to proclaim rights, if at the same time everything were not done to ensure the duty of respecting them by all people, everywhere, and for all people. *Inalienable* insofar as no one can legitimately deprive another person, whoever they may be, of these rights, since this would do violence to their nature."[18]

Human rights are the moral expectations related to the freedom from interference of others and thus are at the base of the moral triangle. They are moral claims grounded on the fact that persons need certain conditions of external freedom and fundamental goods to live and grow. Human rights are the foundation for the good life and life in society. The term "foundation" here is helpful. Think of a foundation of a building. It holds the structure in place and allows for stable structure. From the outside we only notice the foundation if it is breaking. What we do notice is the walls of the building. Human rights "hold" up morality in the same way. Acceptance of and respect for the rights of others is a basic feature of a person with a strong moral identity.

Morality and the Freedom to Choose Goods

The paragraphs above note the importance of social conditions and the importance of others' activities on your life. But morality is not merely about how others ought to respect your rights; it is how you live your life and your relationships and the goods you choose to direct your actions and your life. Morality is a set of expectations about behavior, yours and others.

Rules

Most everyone would acknowledge that at a basic level, morality is about limiting or encouraging particular behaviors. Almost every dictionary, for example, defines morality primarily by rules or standards. Put simply: Actions that violate the rules are wrong. Actions that follow rules are right. At this basic level, morality is quite straightforward. The moral person is responsible for learning the rules and following the rules.

The best-known example of a list of moral rules is the biblical Ten Commandments (Exod. 20:2-17 and Deut. 5:6-21). Here is a common form in which they have been taught:[19]

> I am the Lord your God:
> you shall not have strange Gods before me.
> You shall not take the name of the Lord your God in vain.
> Remember to keep holy the Lord's Day.
> Honor your father and your mother.
> You shall not kill.
> You shall not commit adultery.
> You shall not steal.
> You shall not bear false witness against your neighbor.
> You shall not covet your neighbor's wife.
> You shall not covet your neighbor's goods.

These rules, most of which are "Do nots," are fairly specific. Not all rules are so particular. When Jesus was asked which of the 613 laws of the Code of the Covenant was the "first," or most important, he responded as follows: "You shall love the Lord your God with all your heart, with all your soul, and with all your mind . . . and the second is like it: You shall love your neighbor as yourself (Matt. 22:34-40).[20] These two rules have traditionally together been referred to as "The Great Commandment." Another example of a moral rule with a rather general scope is from Thomas Aquinas. Aquinas stated that the first principle of morality is, "Good is to be done and pursued, and evil is to be avoided."[21] In other words, "Do good and avoid evil." Aquinas believed that all other moral rules, and he certainly held there to be other moral rules, are derived from this overriding rule.

Some discussions of rule-based morality use words other than "rules" to capture the idea that morality is primarily about particular actions (for example, do not kill) or a person's internal disposition that ought or ought not to lead to particular actions (for example, do not covet). Thus we hear language like "commandments," "moral norms," "moral principles," or "moral directives." While there may be some distinctions between these words, for simplicity's sake, we will refer to all of these as moral rules.

Think about the importance of rules for a moment. The experience of driving a car is helpful here. Every moment we drive we face expectations: "Do this and do not do that." There are speed limits, specific driving lanes (stay on the right side), stop signs, yield signs, that allow you to go where you want to go amid the many other people who are going where they want to go. What if there were no traffic laws? Total freedom to drive any way you wanted would result in social chaos. Rules in driving, like rules in life, provide order, and in many situations, order is a very good thing!

Moral rules, however, provide more than just order and stability. Rules can define a minimal sense of identity. They can bind groups. They can also make daily life easier because basic questions have already been answered. Rules are vital to morality and thus are the "second" side of the triangle moving up from the base of human rights.

In the first chapter of this book, we reflected on the creation stories and the notion that persons were created "in the image of God." You will recall the concluding remarks about the responsibility and dignity of persons from those stories. In the first part of this chapter we read about human freedom and the ways in which we experience freedom. Freedoms give us certain powers and thus responsibilities. Because persons have these freedoms, because they are created in the image of God, we know that they ought to be treated in particular ways. Thus when we understand Maya Angelou's use of metaphorical language, we are saddened by the singing of the bound, tied, and imprisoned "person." All of this points to the primary rule in moral theology. We are to recognize all humans as persons.

Recognizing the personhood of others means respecting their rights. But it means much more than that. It means acknowledging them in their likeness to you as well as in their uniqueness as individuals. Every human you meet is a person. This, is, however, not simply about perception. It is not merely how we "see" others. It is about our personal response to their personhood. You experience your personhood most fully when you share yourself in relationships with others.

Intentions/Goals

In his poem *Mending Wall*, Robert Frost describes how he and his neighbor meet once a year to fix the stone wall (or fence) that divides their properties. Frost is not so keen on the wall and indeed wonders why they have it at all. In one part of the poem Frost says he wants to tear the wall down but his neighbor keeps saying, "Good fences make good neighbors." Theologian John Mahoney uses this poem as he reflects on the role of rules in morality. He suggests that moral laws are something like the stone wall in Frost's poem. Mahoney writes, "There is a place for walls, so long as one can answer a few questions first."[22] In other words, there is place for rules, but we have to ask a few questions first. Like, why do they exist? Where did they come from? What are their advantages and limitations? As there is a place for walls and fences, there is a place for rules in the moral life.

Rules are basic to morality, but as you know in your own life, morality contains more than rules. This seems to be a simple point that is sometimes missed in the discussion of morality. Many philosophers, theologians and policymakers seem interested in following the great German philosopher Immanuel Kant and finding the "single principle from which one can generate all and only obligatory actions."[23] Charles Taylor, however, points out significant problems with this view. He notes that our moral life can never be adequately captured in a rule or set of rules.[24] He gives several reasons for this, including the practical one that no set of rules can fit the various situations we find ourselves in every day. Yet his strongest critique of a rule-only morality is that rules, even the best ones, can never become the ground for our own deepest sense of meaning and moral goodness. He argues that we cannot and should not define the center of moral and spiritual lives with rules. "We should," he continues, "find the centre of our spiritual lives beyond the code, deeper than the code, in networks of living concern, which are not to be sacrificed to the code, which must even from time to time subvert it."[25]

Generally speaking, rules exist for reasons beyond themselves. They exist for purposes. While morality includes rules, it is fundamentally more about the purpose than the rule itself. To quote Mahoney, morality is about the "things beyond or behind" the rules, and ultimately, morality is about things that are the "center of meaning" in our lives.

What is "beyond" rules? Primarily *intentions*. Intentions refer to the internal "movement of the will" in persons that leads them to particular actions. Intentions are tied to goals and goods. Goals and goods (we can use them interchangeably here) are the things that "we are after in doing what we do."[26] Intentions, internal to you, and goals, external to you, are inseparable.

Let's reflect on this for a moment. What are the three most important things in your life? For most people, the answer would include interpersonal relationships, friendships, and family. It is important for you to be a good friend or a good spouse or a good parent or a good son or a good daughter. While there are "rules" for this, you know it takes more than following rules to be a good friend. Interpersonal relationships are "goods;" they are notable, necessary, and life-directing objectives in life. We direct our lives, through our intentions, to these goods and we evaluate our lives on our relation to these goods. Robert Frost's neighbor is only partially correct. Good fences may indeed make good neighbors, but so do block parties!

Interpersonal relationships, while perhaps the primary goods in your life, are not the only type of goods in your life. Perhaps you are committed to life in a church or committed to keeping your neighborhood safe. Perhaps you are committed to stopping global climate change or to ending poverty or homelessness in your area. Perhaps you want to make war or abortion less likely, or to see to it that all children get vaccinated and obtain basic medical care. Perhaps you do things to end racism or discrimination in society. Since you are

internally moved to work toward these goods, you set goals for yourself. That is to say, your intentions lead you. You will, for example,
join a group that seeks to end homelessness or you will make a finan-
cial contribution to a group that seeks to end racism.

Maybe at this time in your life, the goods you seek are less gran-
diose. Perhaps you simply want to get high grades and an education,
so as to get a decent job. Perhaps you want to stay healthy and in
physical shape. All of these goods and the goals within them, from
interpersonal relations to communal and professional development,
are crucial elements of moral reflection. Your actions here all stem
from your intentions.

If there is one intention/goal that has risen to prominence in
contemporary moral theology it is sustainability. The moral expectation of sustainability has developed from the realization of three
things:

1. That human activity, particularly the production and consumption of goods, has immense consequences on the earth's resources
   and the basic life systems of the earth (water, air, soil, and climate).

2. That the goods of the earth have value independent of their usefulness for humans.

3. That future generations have a general and indirect moral claim
   on us to leave the earth with appropriate resources and a prosper-
   ous environment for their well being and flourishing.

Sustainability begins with the intention to use natural resources
responsibly to meet human need today without harming the flourishing for future generations and the basic integrity of the earth.
These two fundamental goals lead to moral rules. Here are three
examples: 1. We ought to appropriately use nonrenewable resources
(this includes reusing or recycling them as efficiently as possible); 2.
In our production and consumption of goods, we ought not to compromise the earth's systems; and 3. We ought to minimize the extinc-
tion rates of plants and animals.

The person intentionally seeking sustainability sees herself more
than simply one who follows rules. She sees herself as a responsible

agent within the community of life in creation. She sees herself as part of creation, not "above" creation. She directs her patterns of consumption from her intention to do good in and for the world.

Intentions/goals are the "third side" of the triangle of moral expectations. Resting on the base, human rights, and on the other side, rules, intentions/goals then forms the basic external view of morality.

In some moral conversations, the intentions/goals language is referred to as ideals. Ideals are goals (external goods) we strive for (internal intentions). We may be successful and achieve these goals. But if we do not achieve them, that does not mean we are moral failures. Our moral self-reflection is based on our sense of how committed we are (our intentions) to the ideal (external good) and how much progress we have made achieving the goal.

In the first part of this chapter, we identified four ways people experience freedom. We called them freedom from interference, freedom for simple goods, freedom for complex goods, and freedom of the heart. We complemented each with an element of morality (except for freedom of the heart, that is the topic of the next section). Freedom from interference is associated with human rights. Both types of freedom for goods are associated with rules and intentions/goals. The point of morality is to create the conditions for human flourishing, integral development (yours and others'—your friends, family, community, society, and environment). Human rights, rules, and goods, both simple and complex, can enhance flourishing. The abuse of rights, bad rules, and mistaken goods, both simple and complex, can harm flourishing.

Morality and Fundamental Freedom

Think of a good person, someone you know personally. Write down the person's name and then write down one or two things that you think make this person good. Your answer is probably simple. You might say, for example, that your good person is caring. By this you mean that she does good things for persons and that she seems to do this all the time. Caring is, for her, a persistent and constant character trait. Her actions seem to flow from within her. In other words, caring is a habit for her.

To paraphrase Aristotle, your good person has emotions and actions appropriate to the contexts she finds herself within. She feels the right feelings at the right times toward the right things and people. She chooses to act on these feelings in the right way for the right reasons. Your good person is, in other words, *good at being a person.* She flourishes in both "being" and "doing."[27] In moral language, she is a person of virtue. A virtue is a deep-seated character trait of a person (a habit) that reflects some foundational feature of personhood. People, for example, are meant to be caring; thus a "good" person cares about others.

If you know some good people, you probably also know some other kinds of people. There probably are some people you do not trust. You would never tell them something in confidence because they probably would not keep it to themselves. There probably are some people you would never go to for a favor. You know them to be selfish. There probably are some people who have hurt you. They may be callous. There probably are some people who you would rather not be with because you do not approve of their racist remarks.

I am not saying that these people are all bad or that they are evil people. I am saying that you have experienced people who have dispositions or attitudes that are "negative." They have "habits of the heart and mind" that often lead them to do things or say things that are rude, destructive, or mean. To use traditional moral language, they have vices. Vices, like virtues, are deep-seated character traits (habits). In contrast to virtues, vices are destructive to human flourishing. They are character flaws. The more vices one has, the more likely we are to think of the person as a "bad" person. These people simply have trouble being people! On the other hand, we are likely to think of a person with many good character traits, that is to say, virtues, as a good person.

An interesting feature about virtue and vice is that they are "contagious." Being with good people tends to "rub off" on you. Being with not-so-good people also tends to rub off on you. For example, we tend to pick up habits and ideas from others, particularly from people with strong personalities. This is why parents are always wondering whom their kids are hanging around with. People, culture, and contexts can and do influence character traits.

A key point here is that with our freedom, particularly our fundamental freedom, we have the ability to be the sort of person we ought to be. That is to say, we can develop character traits, either positive or negative. You have a power to make choices about your internal dispositions. For example, are you caring? More importantly, do you want to be caring? Or, are you patient? Do you want to be patient? Are you hard working? Do you want to be hard working? Are you generous or stingy? I once remarked to a friend that I thought he was very optimistic. He thanked me, telling me that he works on it. Growing up, he said, his family was negative and pessimistic.

Virtue

So what are these virtues and vices? The New Testament offers a few lists. In the Gospel of Mark, we read Jesus challenging the religious leaders of his day on several issues, including what one is allowed to eat. Jesus proclaims that it is not what a person puts into his or her body that defiles, but what comes out of a person's heart that defiles. In doing so he lists a set of negative character traits and actions. Jesus says, "For it is from within, from the human heart, that evil intentions come: fornication, theft, murder, adultery, avarice, wickedness, deceit, licentiousness, envy, slander, pride, folly. All these evil things come from within, and they defile a person" (Mark 7:21–22).

St. Paul frequently lists sets of virtues and vices. In his Letter to the Galatians, he contrasts the character traits of those who live by the "works of the flesh" with those who live by the "fruit of the Spirit." He writes, "Now the works of the flesh are obvious: fornication, impurity, licentiousness, idolatry, sorcery, enmities, strife, jealousy, anger, quarrels, dissensions, factions, envy, drunkenness, carousing, and things like these." Later he writes that we ought "not to become conceited, competing against one another, envying one another." He continues, "By contrast, the fruit of the Spirit is love, joy, peace, patience, kindness, generosity, faithfulness, gentleness, and self-control" (Gal. 5:19–22, 26, 22–23).

The traditional list of virtues in moral theology is faith, hope, love, prudence, temperance, justice, and courage. The first three, the "theological virtues," come from Paul's First Letter to the Corinthians (13:13), and the remaining are the classic virtues found in Plato's *Republic* (Book 4). Early Christian theologians, primarily Ambrose and Augustine, incorporated these virtues into moral theology. The theological virtues indicate an acceptance of God and God's grace in our lives. The classic virtues hold that persons can develop these characteristics themselves and, more importantly, persons can develop the conditions and relationships where these characteristics can flourish in others. The traditional list of vices in moral theology is pride, envy, wrath, sloth, greed, gluttony, and lust.

A dominant virtue in contemporary moral theology is solidarity. Its prominence is the result of the place it has in the teaching of Pope John Paul II. Solidarity arises from the realization of three things:

1. The interconnectedness and interdependence (economic, political, ecological) of humanity in the contemporary age;

2. The fact that this interdependence fosters and is built on basic inequalities grounded on "various forms of exploitation, oppression, and corruption;"[28]

3. That the victims of systematic degradation, called the "structures of sin,"[29] are neighbors to us. Each person has basic rights and a "fundamental equality with everyone else" and is, in fact, the "living image of God."[30]

Solidarity is the habit of heart and mind enabling the virtuous person to love the oppressed, to serve the exploited, to sacrifice for the poor, and to give oneself for the good of the others in the work of purifying and transforming social structures, particularly "laws, market regulations, and juridical systems."[31] In sum, "It is a firm and persevering determination to commit oneself to the common good."[32]

Habits

A virtue is a character trait. A character trait is a habit. A habit is an action repeated over time so that the action becomes, in a way, part of the person. The habit becomes so much a part of a person that she is that way without thinking about it. The famous phrase used by Cicero (and repeated by Thomas Aquinas and many others) to describe this is that these habits become "like a second nature" in us.[33] There are at least four types of habits related to morality and human development, four types of patterns of behavior that have the potential to become second nature to us. Only one of the four is specifically moral. The other three contribute to and support morality.

The first type of habits related to morality, like the freedom for simple goods, refers to basic behavioral actions that benefit your health, safety, and basic well-being. Let's call them *personal habits*. If you want to be healthy, for example, you should brush and floss your teeth everyday. You should eat a good breakfast. You should get exercise. For the well-being of others, you should get into the habit of covering your mouth when you cough. By the way, you should look both ways when you cross the street. This first type of habit refers to physical characteristics to keep us healthy and strong (as well as handsome and beautiful and other "good" traits). Do an internet search on "healthy habits" and you are likely to find many such lists.

There are also personal habits that are not helpful or even destructive to us as persons. Some students are habitually late for class. Some people drink too much alcohol and others smoke. Many of us have bad habits and we know they are hard to break. Personal habits are related to morality because they can have an impact on our flourishing and our relationships. We have a moral responsibility to care for ourselves. Our lives are a gift from God and we are called to develop them.

The second form of habits related to morality concerns the choices we make on complex goods. They reflect deeper concerns and commitments and are really habits of the "heart and mind." These habits are "enduring traits of character that persons must possess if they are to be able to sustain a course of activity."[34] That is to say, if you want to do something well, you must develop these habits. We can call these *performance habits* because they are focused on producing character traits needed to accomplish some task well. [35]

According to some sources, if you want to be an expert at anything, you have to put in ten thousand hours—basically, twenty hours a week for ten years.[36] Whether or not the ten thousand hour rule is accurate, in order to do something well, you must put in the time, and to put in the time demands some underlying commitments or goals. But it is not just the time invested in that counts, it is the habits of the heart and mind of the person, for example "diligence, best effort, perseverance, critical thinking and positive attitude"[37] that keeps her on task. Performance habits, traits you need to succeed in an activity (sports/music/business/school), are certainly related to morality and human flourishing, but are not moral in the strict sense. They are more about doing and accomplishing things than being full and true persons. These habits alone, like the habit of brushing your teeth everyday, by themselves do not make one a "good" person. Criminals can be thoughtful, hard working, and diligent in their lives.

The third form of habits consists of those that develop the personhood of the individual and the person in relation to others. These are *moral virtues* properly understood, such as honesty, trustworthiness, and caring for others.

While looking both ways before you cross the street and perseverance are good habits, they are not moral habits or *virtues* strictly understood. Go back to your good person and their characteristics. You may have said your person was good because she was hard working, but you probably said something like she cares or she is loving or she is generous or she puts others above herself. These habits lead to the fundamental characteristics of persons in relationships and are at the center of personal flourishing.

Moral virtue, by its nature, opens us up to our personhood. It pushes us to recognize our uniqueness and our autonomy as well as our basic humanness and our relationality. With virtue we experience internal as well as external unity. Internally, we recognize the connection between our feelings, thoughts, and actions. Externally, we come to understand the multiple of relationships to which we belong. Moral virtue opens us up to giving and receiving love. It makes us at once ready to put the needs of others over our needs, and at the same time it allows us to be vulnerable and able receive the love of others. The point here is that moral virtues, like solidarity, push us to be good at being persons.

We have virtues and vices because we hold some core set of beliefs and commitments in our "heart." These commitments may be religious or not. They may be selfish; they may be limited; they may be broad and expansive. Whatever they are, they ultimately provide the foundation for our moral life. These commitments, expressed as character traits, give a basic wholeness or integrity to our lives. They make us predictable in some fundamental ways.[38] You know your friend is caring. He was caring yesterday and he will probably be caring tomorrow. You know your sister is patient. She was patient yesterday and will probably be patient tomorrow. Character traits, however, are not deterministic. We are not robots. They do not themselves determine exactly what we will do.[39] They do, however, give dominant directions in our lives as they provide the conditions for the possibilities of our action.

The fourth form of habits is *spiritual habits.* These habits include the practices of contemplation, reflection, meditation, and prayer (in its various forms). Such practices spring from something deep within persons and in response to particular experiences of reality. Theologian James Gustafson nicely describes this as "an attitude or disposition of respect, awe, and even devotion that is evoked by human experience of dependence on powers we do not create and cannot fully master."[40] The experience is fundamentally a feeling, rather than a rationalistic experience. Allied with the recognition of dependence is gratitude, which is perhaps the key affection at the core of the spiritual habits. Gratitude is a response to the sense that "the deepest necessary conditions for human flourishing are not created by man, but given."[41] There are, of course, other deep affections here. From these experiences one develops a sense of obligation, remorse for failures, a basic hope, and a sense of direction in life. All these senses fuel and support the moral virtues.

Traditionally, as we saw above, these spiritual habits have been called the Theological Virtues: faith, hope, and love (charity). They are not "true" virtues because we cannot achieve them on our own. We are dependent on God and God's love for us. They are like virtues for two reasons. First, they require our free response to God's initiative. Second, they perfect us as persons.

In summary, morality is as much about character traits, that is to say habits, as it is about particular behavior. To a certain extent we can develop these traits. Some traits are positive and good (some people today might label these as "healthy" traits) and other traits are bad (or, again to use contemporary language, "unhealthy" traits). The traditional language for this is virtue and vice. There are then two constant and persistent questions in moral theology: "*What should I do?*" and "*What sort of person should I be?*"

We have now described the four elements of our triangle of moral theology: the base of human rights; the sides of moral rules and appropriate intentions/goals; and finally, the interior of habitual dispositions and attitudes, virtues.

Morality of the Heart

The chapter started with a discussion of the four types of freedom people experience. The first type was described as "external" freedom or freedom from the interference of others. The other three were described as "internal" freedoms, namely, the powers to choose simple and complex goods and the power to choose the sort of person one wants to be. *It is the burden of the morally mature person (or the morally serious institution or morally responsible community) to appropriate these internal freedoms in their own lives and to promote, as they can, the external freedom of others.*

The second part of the chapter discussed the basic elements of morality, namely rights, rules, intentions/goods, and virtue. *It is the burden of the morally mature person (or the morally serious institution or morally responsible community) to appropriate these elements in their lives.* Promoting and respecting human rights is a foundation. Understanding, weighing, and balancing the set of expectations for behavior and character, however, is the task all of us have as we come to understand ourselves as persons and persons within institutions and communities.

Many people and institutions are, and indeed have to be, rule-based. A primary moral question is then, "Are we breaking or following a rule in this situation?" Some persons or institutions tend to focus not on individual actions but on intentions and goals. Primary moral questions are then, "What are the purposes of your actions?" and "What do you hope to achieve?" Other persons or institutions aim to be directed by virtue. A primary moral concern then is to foster certain "habits of the heart and mind" so as to unify actions and goals in a particular manner.

Most people would argue for the priority of virtue over rules and intentions/goals. The most important moral question in your life is then, "What kind of person am I?" That is to say, "What are my fundamental character traits?" In the end morality is more about being certain "sorts of" persons (or certain "sorts of" institutions) than it is "doing or not doing certain sorts of actions." Particular actions and the rules are, nevertheless, very important. Rules "can be the eyes of virtue. They can help us notice aspects of a situation we might otherwise miss, and they can point us in the direction we ought to go."[42] Even the fully virtuous (and how many of us are?) need some rule-based direction, "eyes" if you will, every once in a while.

The priority of virtue seems to shift in organizations and communities where "goodness" and "right and wrong" actions tend to be measured in goals achieved. Yet organizations often do strive to build particular "cultures" or work environments that reflect various "habits of the heart and mind." The virtue-based questions then become, "What kind of institution are we?" "What do we value?" "What ideals are we committed to?" In the end, morality is about actions, intentions, and character traits and the proportional understanding of them in life. We live this in relationships, institutions, and communities. Thus it is critical to foster relationships, institutions, and communities that create the conditions for human development and flourishing.

Think about this. If you want to get married, what characteristics might you look for in a future spouse? You would want him or her to have a developed sense of responsibility and duty in life. You would want the person to be responsible to you, the family, the workplace, and to the larger community. Being responsible includes acting appropriately in particular situations. This means at least two things, respecting the basic rights of others and following general behavioral expectations (rules). Third, you would want a person who has developed goals in life, who realizes the consequences of actions are at times as important as actions themselves. Finally, and most importantly, you want a person of integrity. You want the person to be honest, faithful, and understanding. You want to marry a person, or indeed be friends with persons, who have a sense of integrating the triangle with its sides of rights, rules, and intentions/goals, as well as its interiority of virtue. Parents want to raise kids who do well on all four of these because in the end, they want their kids to be "good."

It is up to persons, institutions, and communities to appropriate rights, rules, intentions/goods, and virtues so as to create the conditions for human flourishing in their own lives, in their families, in their workplaces, in their many communities and indeed to ensure the prospect for flourishing for future generations. This is one of the many demands on the morality of the heart.

Moral Identity

The introduction to this book suggested that we ought to study moral theology through the "gate" of seven clusters of ideas. Chapter 1 examined the first cluster, namely the way people talk about morality. The present chapter considered the cluster of the experiences of freedom and the cluster of the fundamental terms in morality. The close reader will have noticed connections. They overlap.

The reflections on freedom could very well have referenced Genesis 1–3. The creation and disobedience stories illustrated the types of freedom that the man and woman had and, analogically, the freedom you have. They were free from external interference, they acted for simple goods (the fruit was said to taste good), and they acted for complex goods (to be like God).

The narrative offers a question to its readers. How do you use your freedom? It suggests the complexities of freedom. On one hand, we ought to do things that will expand our experience of freedom for complex goods. This can be done through education (formal and informal), relationships (intimate and casual), travel, and so on, when combined with a sense of reflection. On the other hand, we ought to do things that focus and direct our freedom. We can, and often do, misuse our freedom. Your moral identity is defined by how much you integrate morality into your life. That is to say, how you use the various types of freedom.

In reflecting on these stories, we noted that the "image of God" theme has two ramifications for moral theology. The first is to affirm the human dignity of persons. When one recognizes this as a descriptive fact of creation, the notion that persons have basic rights follows. The second ramification of the image of God theme is that persons are relational and responsible. We, in a sense, fulfill our dignity when we, like God, give to others, nurture others, and sustain others as part of reaching a union or relationality with them. Moral rules, intentions/goals, and virtues, in the end, direct us toward this.

Your moral identity is expressed then in your various relationships and indeed in the times you choose not to create relationships or to end relationships. Your moral identity is also expressed in the rules you choose to follow (most telling, perhaps, are the rules you choose not to follow), your many intentions/goals in life, and your deep-seated habits of the heart and mind.

Questions

1. Describe the four senses of freedom and give examples of your experience of each.

2. Describe the difference between "freedom *from*" something and "freedom *for*" something. What is the relationship between "freedom *from*" and "freedom *for*?" Which is more important in your life? Explain.

3. Describe the four elements of morality (rights, rules, intentions/goals, virtues). Which is more important in your life? Explain.

4. What is meant by "situated freedom?" Describe the nature of freedom and the experience of it in real-life situations.

5. Describe your sense of morality in the following way. Part one: What is the most important right in your life? Give one reason why it is the most important right for you. What is the most important rule in your life? Give one reason why it is the most important rule for you. What is the most important intention/goal in your life? Give one reason why it is the most important intention/goal for you. What is the most important virtue in your life? Give one reason why it is the most important virtue for you. Part two: What is the thing or idea in your mind that holds the right, rule, intention/goal, and virtue together? Explain.

6. This book is about moral theology and, not surprisingly, the author uses biblical and other religious sources to develop ideas. The author also uses nonreligious sources to develop ideas. Discuss how and why the author uses nonreligious sources in this chapter.

CHAPTER THREE

Relationality and Love

The Samaritan who helped the Jew on the Jericho Road was "good" because he responded to the human need that he was presented with . . . Saint Paul assures us that the loving act of redemption was done "while we were yet sinners"—that is, at the point of our greatest need for love. Since the white man's personality is greatly distorted by segregation, and his soul is greatly scarred, he needs the love of the Negro. The Negro must love the white man, because the white man needs his love to remove his tensions, insecurities, and fears.

—Martin Luther King Jr.[1]

He has told you, O mortal, what is good; and what does the Lord require of you but to do justice, and to love kindness, and to walk humbly with your God.   —Micah 6:8

The best-known of Jesus' stories is the parable of the Good Samaritan. It is a narrative that at once surprises and animates people. Dr. King's reflection on it above is fully in line with Jesus' original telling of it—the parable demands a surprising if not shocking love. The second quotation is from the prophet Micah in the Old Testament. The chapter in which this quote appears begins stating that God has a controversy with the people (6:2) because they have forgotten God. God reminds them of His saving history. Micah tries to make amends with God and asks what the people should now do. Should they offer sacrifices and bow down to God? The response is simple, direct, and powerful. Indeed one might say it is a summary of moral theology: You know what is good—always act with justice, always love kindness (be compassionate and love being compassionate), and humbly "walk" with God in you life. This chapter is about love, the fundamental issue in moral theology. It addresses love both as an organizing principle that holds the aspects of moral theology together and as the basic expectation of character and action in the Christian moral life.

The Structure of Moral Theology

Moral theology is a systematic look at morality. Recall our description of morality *as a set of expectations aimed to enhance the flourishing of persons, relationships, communities, and environments.* This description invites several questions. The first is, "Where do these expectations ultimately come from?" Another is, "How does one live out these expectations?" Thirdly, and perhaps most importantly, "Why do I have to follow these expectations?" Moral theology, as a systematic look at morality, attempts to answer these (and other) questions. This discussion will begin with a general description of where moral theology "comes from." It is an exercise in ethical discourse.

Moral theology has a characteristic intellectual or rational design. There are two ways to talk about this structure. The first is a "flow-chart" view and the second is a "peeling-away" view. To prepare for the first, think of writing on a blackboard. You draw four boxes, one on top of the other, and then draw an arrow leading from each box to the one below it. To prepare for the second view, think of peeling through the layers of an onion, or better yet, a golf ball or baseball, to get through the levels and eventually reach the core. Either way, the structure of moral theology includes ideas about God (theology), ideas about humanity (anthropology), expectations of behavior and character (morality), and appropriation (persons making choices). Historically, this structure of moral theology has been labeled "natural law." It is called this as it highlights the God-given nature of humans, including the human ability to reason about what it means to be human. In contemporary moral theology, this structure is often referred to as "personalism."

The "flow-chart" view is a top-down model that begins with the source of moral thinking and moves to the particular application of that thinking. We begin with the more remote idea and make our way to the more pressing issue. Here is the view when we look at the system of moral theology from this perspective: Moral theology begins with theology and moves to anthropology; from the anthropology comes the morality that persons and communities are then to appropriate.

We can explore this in more detail. The design of moral theology begins with a theology. Theology, put simply, means statements about God. Moral theology ultimately is based on beliefs about the nature of God and God's purposes for persons and creation. Characteristic language here is, "God is . . ." or "God desires . . ." or "God intends . . ." or "God does, . . ." Stated in general terms, moral expectations come from an understanding of God, but they do not come directly from theology. There is a second and mediating stage.

The second stage in moral theology is an anthropology. Anthropology here refers to the understanding of what it means to be a person. Persons (all of us) are certain sorts of beings. Characteristic language here is, "The person is . . ." or "Humans are . . ." or "Persons have. . . ." As we have seen earlier in this book, Genesis chapters 1–3 is an important source for understanding personhood in the Christian tradition.

Moral expectations, the third stage, come from the theologically based anthropology. Morality "begins" with the basic experience of the self as a person and the related experience of others as persons, that is to say, when one experiences the anthropology. It continues with the realization that my flourishing depends on others and that the flourishing of others depends on me. But more than that, it continues with the realization that flourishing happens within certain conditions. Morality is then about the expectations (the rights, rules, intentions/goals, and virtues, the "Do this" or "Don't do that" or "Be this" and "Do not be that") that are thought to be the conditions for this flourishing.

I want to make an important distinction here: Morality is for persons. We have no moral expectations of plants or animals or natural resources. We may have moral expectations of persons, however, in their relationships with plants, animals, and natural resources. To put it another way, persons alone are the subject of morality, because only persons can be moral actors in the true sense. Only persons have moral responsibility. However, persons as well as plants, animals, and natural resources can be the object of morality. Animals, plants, and natural resources cannot be virtuous. They may have some instinctual inclinations or goals, and indeed those inclinations may cause harm to humans and other animals, but we do not call this morality. Some animals might respond to rudimentary rules in their communities, but, again, if they break such a "rule," we do not consider them to be immoral. And yet, animals or perhaps whole species may indeed be said to have moral claims, that is to say, rights, against persons.

The final stage of the structure of moral theology is the individual and communal appropriation of the morality. It is here that the practices of reflection, prayer, and good decision-making processes are vital. We are reminded of the often-cited teaching of Paul VI. He notes that individual persons and communities must objectively analyze their situation and context, know the basic moral expectations, and apply those to the context.[2] In the words of John XXIII, there are three basic stages for putting moral expectations into practice: "First, one reviews the concrete situation; secondly, one forms a judgment on it in the light of these same principles; thirdly, one decides what in the circumstances can and should be done to implement these principles. These are the three stages that are usually expressed in the three terms: look, judge, act."[3] The last chapter considers conscience, and will address decision making in more detail.

To summarize, the architecture of moral theology begins with theology and then moves to anthropology. From reflection on the anthropology comes morality. It is the burden of the person or communities to appropriate the expectations for behavior and character. An example illustrating the structure of moral theology presented in the "flow-chart" method here and the role love plays as a unifying feature is appropriate. The text selected below is an excerpt from *Gaudium et Spes*. The importance of *Gaudium et Spes* for moral theology, indeed for the whole of Catholic life, cannot be overstated. It is one of most important documents from the Second Vatican Council,[4] which is itself the most important event in the church in the last 150 years.[5] The text, paragraph #24 (cited by John Paul II as crucial to his own intellectual project[6]), is central to *Gaudium et Spes*. Note the progression of the thinking and the role that love plays in this thinking.

Theology: God, who has fatherly concern for everyone, has willed that all men should constitute one family and treat one another in a spirit of brotherhood.

Anthropology: For having been created in the image of God, who "from one man has created the whole human race and made them live all over the face of the earth" (Acts 17:26), all men are called to one and the same goal, namely God himself. Indeed, the Lord Jesus, when He prayed to the Father, "that all may be one ... as we are one" (John 17:21–22) opened up vistas closed to human reason. For He implied a certain likeness between the union of the divine Persons, and the unity of God's sons in truth and charity.

Morality: For this reason, love for God and neighbor is the first and greatest commandment. Sacred Scripture, however, teaches us that the love of God cannot be separated from love of neighbor: "If there is any other commandment, it is summed up in this saying: Thou shalt love thy neighbor as thyself.... Love therefore is the fulfillment of the Law" (Rom. 13:9–10; cf. 1 John 4:20). This likeness [the Triune God] reveals that man, who is the only creature on earth which God willed for itself, cannot fully find himself except through a sincere gift of himself (cf. Luke 17:33).

Appropriation: To men growing daily more dependent on one another, and to a world becoming more unified every day, this truth [that is to say "love"] proves to be of paramount importance. [7]

The theology in this quotation is short and admittedly insufficient, but one can nevertheless see the role that it plays in directing morality. Christians believe that God has loving concern for all and that God intends for all persons to be one family (theology). This matters for: 1. How we see people (anthropology) and 2. How we treat people (morality). The basis of Christian morality is that *God loves*.

The anthropology section is also in need of deeper explanation, yet it contains basic truths that Christians hold about humans and human nature: Persons are created in the image of God, persons have distinctiveness as individuals, persons have a fundamental orientation to be united with God, and persons know God's will through reason and Scripture.

The reference to persons as the "image" of God (Gen. 1:26–27) is perhaps the most cited biblical text used to describe Christian anthropology. The key phrase in that text is that God created "humankind," male and female, in the image and likeness of God. There are differences in humans, but no human difference overrides the image of God in persons. Indeed, the differences illustrate this image all the more powerfully.[8] As was said in the first chapter of this book: The common and highly accepted understanding of "image and likeness" of God, from the pope to biblical scholars, is that it means that persons were created to be God's responsible representatives on earth. When blessing the couple, God commissions them to be something like a manager in a relationship with an owner— thus the "dominion" God gives them is to care for creation as its creator would care for it.

An equally important anthropological claim is that all persons are called to be with God. The common end of persons, as well as the common creation in God's image, unites individuals in common personhood. As the text points out, God is three Persons, a Trinity. That is to say, God is a relational being in the external sense and the internal sense. Humans image this relational God in their own relationships of truth and love.

There is another way of looking at this structure that begins with that which is closest to us and moves to the more abstract. If the first explanation of the structure of moral theology is the "flow-chart" view, this second view is the "peeling away" view. Simply stated, moral reflection does not begin in the abstract. It begins in real life. This second view of the structure goes like this: A person has to make a decision. The person has to act. In the last paragraph, this was referred to as an *appropriation* of morality for the particular context. The person then "peels away" the particularities of a situation to "look for" *morality,* that is to say, the expectations of behavior and character. When asked why the person chose to act in such a way, the person, in a sense, "peels away" another layer to look for the justification and meaning behind moral expectations. When pushed to this end, the next layer is an understanding of being a person. This is characteristic of both religiously and nonreligiously based morality. All morality is supported in some way by an *anthropology.* The "peeling" can continue and the person asks more "Why?" questions, until one gets to the level of the basic and ultimate commitment that ground a sense of morality. In religious morality one ultimately gets to the core, that from which there is no more "peeling away." Therefore, the foundation of the anthropology is a *theology,* an understanding of God as the ground of all being.

In short, the moral choice is an application or appropriation of morality (expectations about behavior and character) which itself is grounded on an understanding of humans, an anthropology. In moral theology, the anthropology is understood within a theological context.

Whether it is considered in the "flow-chart" style (theology informs an anthropology which forms a morality that directs choice) or in the "peel-away" style (a choice is made from morality which is grounded on an anthropology which is based on theology), the glue that holds the structure together in moral theology is always love.

Love is central and foundational to moral theology. Love is an "end in itself" that points to a higher reality. In other words, to love and experience love is good without reference to ends or consequences and, at the same time, as you love and experience love, you participate in something greater than your love. The next section of this chapter, also considering the "structure" of moral theology, looks at the overall theological and anthropological theme that directs morality, namely, the life and teaching of Jesus.

The Kingdom of God as the Organizing Theme of Morality

It is usual practice in moral theology to reflect on particular biblical passages and to consider their relevance. In this book, for example, we looked at the creation stories. A more thorough approach to using the Bible in moral theology explores broad and comprehensive biblical themes. This section will take this approach as it describes the general features of morality, the set of expectations about persons' character and behavior.

The main theme in the story of Jesus is the kingdom, or the reign, of God.[9] Scripture scholar Gerhard Lohfink writes, it was for this "that Jesus lived. For its sake he gave his all. He spoke of nothing else."[10] But what Jesus meant by the kingdom of God and how it is to be understood in the present day are matters of debate.

In Jesus' time, the Israelites lived under the sword of Caesar's kingdom, the Roman Empire. But this had not always been the case. There was a time in their history when they were themselves a kingdom, and many of Jesus' contemporaries looked back on that time as a golden age. They also looked forward to a time when they would have their own kingdom again. When Jesus preached the kingdom, he must have evoked strong feelings from the people. Indeed, there must have been people who thought he was "declaring the restoration of an Israel free from outside domination."[11]

If the people of Jesus' time thought living in a kingdom was the normal state of affairs, the people of today do not. As a product of a democratic culture, I have never lived in a kingdom nor do I ever hope to live in a (political) kingdom. My guess is that most people in the West and maybe people generally do not long to live in a society characterized by lordship, kingship, and dominion. The language of "kingdom" today seems both archaic and oppressive. However, when we review what Jesus meant by the kingdom of God, we see a kingdom very different from that experienced by the people of his time and, indeed, a kingdom very different from our modern connotations.

There are two things to know about Jesus' teaching of the kingdom. First, it is not geographical or territorial. The kingdom is not a place on the map. It is better understood as an activity or presence of God in the world; thus some commentators prefer the word "reign" of God. But the idea of the reign of God does not fully capture Jesus' teaching. The kingdom of God is not simply the activity of God in the world, it is rather the reign of God being accepted and lived out, appropriated (to use a word we used in this book), by persons. The kingdom is, in a sense, made possible by the behavior and character traits of persons following the behavior and character traits of Jesus. As Jesus says, "You are the salt of the earth" (Matt. 5:13), and "You are the light of the world" (Matt. 5:14). At the same time, the growth of the kingdom can become stagnated by behaviors and character traits of persons. We are, as we learned from the first two chapters of Genesis, God's responsible representatives on earth and we can, as we learned from the third chapter of Genesis, deny that we are God's responsible representatives on earth.

What then is the kingdom of God for Jesus? Let's begin with a reflection by Lohfink comparing Jesus' teaching on the kingdom to utopian thinking.

> Utopia almost always demands a total or at least a closed system. Therefore the old world must first be demolished. But with Jesus the tensions within reality are maintained: the fruitful tension between the state, which Jesus did not fundamentally question (Mark 12:17), and the people of God; the tension between the individual and the community; between the *already* of the reign of God and its *not yet*; and finally the tension between grace and freedom, that is, between the reign of God as pure gift and the fact that human beings can work in freedom and yet with ultimate passion for the reign of God. He did not destroy any of these tensive arcs; he maintained them. Jesus was very well aware of the "impossibility" of God's cause in the world, but he knows that God's possibilities are infinitely greater than all human possibilities (Mark 10:27).[12]

A key description of the kingdom in the Gospels is that it is "already" but "not yet." It is present in the life of Jesus (see Luke 11:20 and 17:21), but will not be fulfilled until the end of time (see Luke 22:30). Thus we live in something of a "middle time," where we catch glimpses of the kingdom or see reflections of its fullness within short openings of time.

In Christian theology there have been at least three reduction-istic views of this "already but not yet" tension in the Gospels. I call these "reductionistic" because they ignore the complexity of the term in favor of simplicity and reduce the kingdom to one of its characteristics. This is important to note here because these interpretations have consequences for how one views moral theology.

The first reductionistic view recognizes only the "not yet" of the kingdom. In this view, kingdom of God simply refers to heaven and the afterlife. This tendency relativizes the moral teachings of Jesus and denigrates active Christian engagement in the world. This is perhaps the "original sin" of Christians. Indeed, it seems that on several occasions even the apostles did not fully understand the kingdom.[13] We partake of the "fruit" of complacency, laziness, complicit silence, indifference, and the supposed impossibility of living out the Gospel, reasoning that Jesus merely asks us to seek heaven.[14] This tendency stands in contrast to the great prayer of Jesus, the prayer that seems to "summarize his whole will."[15]

> Our Father in heaven,
> hallowed be your name.
> Your kingdom come.
> Your will be done,
> on earth as it is in heaven.
> Give us this day our daily bread.
> And forgive us our debts,
> as we also have forgiven our debtors.
> And do not bring us to the time of trial,
> but rescue us from the evil one.
>   —Matthew 6:9–13

In this prayer, perhaps the most popular prayer in Christianity, Christians do not pray to go to heaven. They are not praying for the "not yet" to be fulfilled in the afterlife. They instead ask for certain types of relationships in their lives and in their communities.[16] The irony of the tendency to stress the "not yet" and forget the "already" is that it actually defers the kingdom. As Lohfink writes, "And that, that alone, is the why 'already' becomes 'not yet.' "[17]

Pope Francis, on the other hand, encourages us to take the "already" of the kingdom seriously. He writes, "Let us believe the Gospel when it tells us that the kingdom of God is already present in this world and is growing, here and there, and in different ways: like the small seed which grows into a great tree (cf. Matt. 13:31-32), like the measure of leaven that makes the dough rise (cf. Matt. 13:33) and like the good seed that grows amid the weeds (cf. Matt. 13: 24-30) and can always pleasantly surprise us. The kingdom is here, it returns, it struggles to flourish anew. . . . May we never remain on the sidelines of this march of living hope!"[18]

The second reductionist tendency, the opposite of the first, is to define the kingdom primarily in terms of the "already." Thus the kingdom is associated with here and now and particular social programs or social arrangements. Identifying an outward legal code, even as it limits evil, with "the presence of God in the world"[19] misses fundamental requirements of personal commitment (love, compassion, forgiveness, active concern for others) crucial to the kingdom and it limits the understandings of God's presence in the world.

The third reductionistic tendency locates the kingdom of God solely "within" the person's heart. The justification for this view is based on a particular translation of Luke 17:21. As we saw above, the kingdom does require certain types of character traits, yet however important virtue is, virtue only captures part of the kingdom. As Jesus says in the Beatitudes (Matt. 5:3-9), we are to be "pure in heart" (an internal trait) but at the same time we must be "peacemakers" (an external relational action). We are to be "poor in spirit" (an internal trait) but at the same time we must be "merciful" (an external relational action). For Jesus, "It is not only individuals and their inner lives that need redeeming but also the situations within which they live. . . .Jesus was not just concerned with souls. He wanted a changed society."[20]

Again quoting Pope Francis:

Reading the Scriptures also makes it clear that the Gospel is not merely about our personal relationship with God. Nor should our loving response to God be seen simply as an accumulation of small personal gestures to individuals in need, a kind of "charity à la carte", or a series of acts aimed solely at easing our conscience. The Gospel is about the kingdom of God (cf. Luke 4:43); it is about loving God who reigns in our world. To the extent that he reigns within us, the life of society will be a setting for universal fraternity, justice, peace, and dignity. Both Christian preaching and life, then, are meant to have an impact on society.[21]

The kingdom is "already and not yet." The Pontifical Biblical Commission nicely describes the implication of the tension.

The future reality of the kingdom invades (and determines) the present situation. The real and definitive destiny of humankind, when evil will have been vanquished, justice reinstated and humanity's craving for life and peace fully satisfied, remains a future experience, but the contours of this future—a future that reveals God's entire purpose for humanity—contribute to defining what human life should be already in the present.[22]

The kingdom has internal and personal expectations as well as external and social expectations. The future, the not yet, "invades" the present. It ought to have an impact on "every dimension of reality . . . soul and body, health and sickness, wealth and poverty, adults and children, family and society."[23]

The Kingdom and the Characteristics of Morality

The Pontifical Biblical Commission, in a recent publication, reviewed the variety of moral teachings in the Bible. It argued that a comparative analysis of these texts provides an overarching view of morality. More specifically, the Commission holds that a scriptural approach to morality is guided by six methodological principles.[24] The principles are: convergence, contrast, advance, community, discernment, and finality. Given that the kingdom of God is the theme of Jesus' life and teachings, and indeed that it appears throughout the New Testament, these principles can provide the approach for thinking about the kingdom and the appropriation of the kingdom.

Convergence

A primary characteristic of the kingdom of God is that it flourishes within creation. Creation finds its source in God, and, as is often confirmed in the Bible, this creation is fundamentally good. The kingdom then does not first demand destruction and revolution. It demands living like God intended persons to live. There is therefore an aspect of the kingdom that claims universality, not in terms of dominance or force, but through serious reflection on personhood, relationality, and living within the world.

Common human experiences of goodness, love, compassion, forgiveness, giving, friendship, family, reconciliation, solidarity, and so on (recall the category of intrinsic goods) are the foundations of the kingdom. The kingdom does not exist anywhere without them. Acting for the kingdom, in whatever form, is essentially "a declaration of belief about the world and the God who created it."[25] These acts are, to use Catholic terminology, sacramental in that they establish "a contact point between the believer and God."[26]

Contrast

The complementary principle to the principle of convergence, the "yin" to the "yang" of convergence, if you will, is that the kingdom challenges some basic social and individual values. In very concrete ways, the kingdom turns commonly held values around and upside down. As Jesus famously said, "So the last will be first, and the first will be last" (Matt. 20:16). In that way the kingdom of God is dramatically different from earthly kingdoms. The kingdom of God is not built on wealth and material things; it rejects greed and consumerism, although it recognizes the relative value and goodness of material things. The kingdom of God does not grow nor does it stay strong nor can it fend off enemies by use of force or violence, war or killing, torture or threat, imprisonment or fear. All these things are contrary to the kingdom. Pope Francis powerfully captures this idea. He writes, the "parable of the weeds among the wheat (cf. Matt. 13:24–30) graphically illustrates [this] . . . the enemy can intrude upon the kingdom and sow harm, but ultimately he is defeated by the goodness of the wheat."[27]

The "mighty" on their thrones, of whatever kind, will not be first in the kingdom, nor will the arrogant or the "proud in their conceit" (Luke 1). As Pope Francis reminds us, Jesus

> was born in a manger, in the midst of animals, like children of poor families; he was presented at the Temple along with two turtledoves, the offering made by those who could not afford a lamb (cf. Luke 2:24; Lev. 5:7); he was raised in a home of ordinary workers and worked with his own hands to earn his bread. When he began to preach the kingdom, crowds of the dispossessed followed him, illustrating his words: "The Spirit of the Lord is upon me, because he has anointed me to preach good news to the poor" (Luke 4:18). He assured those burdened by sorrow and crushed by poverty that God has a special place for them in his heart: "Blessed are you poor, yours is the kingdom of God" (Luke 6:20); he made himself one of them: "I was hungry and you gave me food to eat", and he taught them that mercy towards all of these is the key to heaven (cf. Matt. 25:5ff.).[28]

The kingdom is far from "already" in situations of exploitation and oppression, prejudice and hate, anger and abuse. The "already" can be experienced as suffering, pain, and agony are diminished. Yet the "already" is realized when followers of Jesus themselves face suffering, pain, and agony in their efforts to alleviate these things in others. Those committed to the kingdom must "invade" those situations, conscious of their means and their end, knowing that their means are nothing more than their ends in process. The "already" is the "not yet" in process. The kingdom then grows and thrives by the living, active, and loving witness of those committed to Jesus.

Advance

God continues to enter the world and to reveal God's self. The revelation of God is like a journey for humanity. The Pontifical Biblical Commission writes, "God enters the world and reveals himself increasingly, he addresses himself to people and provokes them to comprehend his will more deeply."[29] Thus we stand today, as the saying goes, on the shoulders of giants, saints, prophets, as well as holy and good people who have perceived this continuing revelation and lived the kingdom in their lives within their contexts. These giants have contributed much to our understanding of the kingdom as they sought the "higher righteousness" Jesus demands (Matt. 5:20) and refined the conscience of their communities. There exists the possibility and indeed the probability of adjustment and refinement in morality. Moral positions may evolve.[30] Moral theology has, for example, advanced its responses to slavery, suicide, relationships to persons of other faiths, war, human rights and freedoms, and capital punishment. These are advances, not simply changes, in moral theology, because they reflect the greater realization of the command to love and a greater expression of the "already" of the kingdom.

Moral rules, moral ideals, and moral virtues are necessary and foundational elements in moral theology, yet they essentially serve the Christian's sense of imitating and following Jesus in the moment, "a way of life that reflects now the future reality of the kingdom."[31]

Community

The philosopher Martha Nussbaum begins one of her books with a narrative from the ancient Greek poet Pindar. According to Nussbaum, Pindar "dedicated his career to writing lyric odes in praise of human excellence."[32] Note that what Pindar calls "human excellence" is what we are calling human flourishing (we could also use the terms integral human development or fulfillment). In one of his poems, Pindar challenges the notion held by his contemporaries that human excellence is something that can be achieved on one's own. Nussbaum, of course, uses this narrative to challenge her contemporaries who think that human goodness is something that can be achieved on one's own. Nussbaum, following Pindar, tells us that the flourishing of the good person, "is like a young plant: something growing in the world, slender, fragile, in constant need of food from without."[33] A plant needs all sorts of external conditions to thrive. "So, the poet suggests, do we."[34] Nussbaum's use of Pindar is helpful. We are like plants. Any parent or teacher knows that their primary responsibility is to nurture children. Where would you be today without the support of your friends and family? But we are not plants. We are autonomous individuals able to direct our actions as we see fit (for simple and complex goods). A full understanding of morality recognizes both our individuality and our relationality. Yet we must not think that our relationality simply means that we depend on others for things and for support. It is much deeper than that. As Nussbaum says, "Even when we do not need the *help* of friends and loved ones, love and friendship still matter to us for their own sake."[35]

Love and friendship "matter to us." This simple statement is so obvious that to state it seems trite. Relationships are the most important things in your life. Theologian Edward Vacek describes well the centrality of relationships for us. He writes:

> Relationships are themselves great goods, and therefore they are worth the time and energy invested in them. Most of us spend countless hours in creating, maintaining, and fostering our relationships. We play with one another, go for walks with one another, talk on the phone just to keep up. We "waste time" together that could be "more profitably spent" were it not for the fact that the relationships we thereby maintain and build are among the highest goods of our lives.[36]

What Vacek describes, and indeed what we all experience, is the significance of the "complex" good of interpersonal relationships. You experience yourself both as individual, a person who can think and feel and act on one's own, and as a person in relation to others. *You are* a brother or sister, son or daughter, friend, neighbor, husband or wife, cousin, and citizen of a city, county, state, and nation. *You are* a member of various groups, for example, clubs or a church or a team or a political party or professional association. Decisions regarding these relationships are the most important decisions we make in life.

You exist within a variety of spheres of relationships and your flourishing is contingent on the well-being of these relationships.

Relationships are at the heart of morality. Morality is fundamentally about *how we are* in these relationships. This fact is a basic feature of moral theology.

All of this points to an important feature about "being" human. We are not only autonomous individuals, we are indeed, to use Pindar's image, like plants. We are by our nature vulnerable along with being autonomous. Cathleen Kaveny is, however, correct in her reflection on our basic vulnerability in life: "It is only during a portion of our lives, and sometimes only during a small portion, that we are relatively independent—yet we remain the same people over the waxing and waning of function."[37] Vulnerability is crucial for good relationships and good relationships provide the conditions for protecting our vulnerability.

Relationships provide the conditions of the possibility for human flourishing. They also can provide the conditions where human flourishing is diminished, limited, and inhibited. All of this is to say that morality includes not only expectations of individuals about character and behavior that are expressed within relationships. Joseph Ratzinger (later Pope Benedict XVI) was correct when he wrote, " 'Morality' is not an abstract code of norms for behavior, but presupposes a community way of life within which morality itself is clarified and is able to be observed. Historically considered, morality does not belong to the area of subjectivity, but is guaranteed by the community and has a reference to the community. . . . Every morality needs its 'we.' "[38] The point here is that morality, generally understood, refers to something beyond or external to the individual person. Moral expectations are initially learned and lived within communities.

It seems almost impossible to speak of human dignity and personal development outside of relationships. Human flourishing happens within relationships and social groups. Families, schools, teams, organizations, clubs, and communities form us. Yet the larger patterns of social relations, political and economic structures, can also enhance our flourishing.

The term often used to describe this is the "common good." The common good is "the sum total of social conditions which allow people, either as groups or as individuals, to reach their fulfillment more fully and more easily. It is the social and community dimension of the moral good."[39] Basic to moral theology is the realization that persons are both autonomous and relational. In the words of the Pontifical Council for Justice and Peace, "The human person cannot find fulfillment in himself, that is, apart from the fact that he exists 'with' others and 'for.'" Thus, "No expression of social life—from the family to intermediate social groups, associations, enterprises of an economic nature, cities, regions, states, up to the community of peoples and nations—can escape the issue of its own common good, in that this is a constitutive element of its significance and the authentic reason for its very existence."[40]

To return to our kingdom of God theme, a kingdom has people. Indeed if there are no people, there is no kingdom. The unity of God calls for the unity of people. So the kingdom of God entails community, but given the diversity of creation, the kingdom is not a simple community of like-minded and similar-looking people. Kingdom building is solidarity building. It is the "determination to commit oneself to the common good . . . a commitment to the good of one's neighbor with the readiness, in the gospel sense, to 'lose oneself' for the sake of the other."[41] Solidarity pushes us to see others not as objects or impersonal beings or faceless humans, but as our neighbors. "One's neighbor is then not only a human being with his or her own rights and a fundamental equality with everyone else, but becomes the living image of God the Father. . . . One's neighbor must therefore be loved, even if an enemy, with the same love with which the Lord loves him or her."[42]

Jesus often used images to describe the kingdom. In the Gospel of Matthew, chapter 13, for example, he speaks of the kingdom as a seed, yeast, and a buried treasure. He also describes it as activities of a farmer, merchant, and fisherman. Following this lead, we too can use images to describe the communal aspect of the kingdom. Theologian Bryan Massingale, in his discussion of race and racism, suggests two that are applicable here: the kingdom as a "welcome table" and the kingdom as the "beloved community." The welcome table suggests hospitality, solidarity, nourishment, fellowship, and equity. This is an image we all can relate to. The beloved community was the organizing moral vision of Dr. Martin Luther King Jr. Quoting the King Center website:

> Dr. King's Beloved Community is a global vision, in which all people can share in the wealth of the earth. In the Beloved Community, poverty, hunger, and homelessness will not be tolerated because international standards of human decency will not allow it. Racism and all forms of discrimination, bigotry and prejudice will be replaced by an all-inclusive spirit of sisterhood and brotherhood. In the Beloved Community, international disputes will be resolved by peaceful conflict resolution and reconciliation of adversaries, instead of military power. Love and trust will triumph over fear and hatred. Peace with justice will prevail over war and military conflict.[43]

These metaphors, that the kingdom is a welcome table or the kingdom is the beloved community, help us image the possibilities of the "already" as it inspires us to actualize the "not yet."

Discernment

To work toward the kingdom requires a prophetic edge and patient work. This takes wisdom to discern the signs of the times and to respond appropriately. Evil must be named and resisted. Good must be proclaimed and witnessed.[44] Morality moves on, decisions must be made; real life is on our doorsteps. The practices of reflection, prayer, and good decision-making processes are vital. These will be discussed more in the next chapter.

Pope Francis reminds us of the importance of patient work when he describes the principle "Time is greater than space." It is important to think about time here, not in the sense of a ticking clock but in the sense of the in between of the "already" and the "not yet." We are attracted to, pulled toward the "not yet" of the fullness of the kingdom. Seeing this allows us to live our lives directed by love and to "work slowly but surely, without being obsessed with immediate results. It helps us patiently to endure difficult and adverse situations, or inevitable changes in our plans." Hoping our lives and choices bear fruit in time we can act "without anxiety, but with clear convictions and tenacity."[45]

It takes thoughtful discernment to fulfill the prayer of Jesus, "Our Father in heaven, hallowed be your name. Your kingdom come. Your will be done, on earth as it is in heaven."

Finality

The kingdom rests on faith and is active in love, but it also is directed by the third theological virtue, hope. The "not yet" of the kingdom is the inspiration, the hope, for action today. Hope reminds us that there is always something more, something beyond. The vision of union with God imprints a profound mark on our actions and indeed on the motivations for our actions.[46] Union of life with God after life, "is impossible without having lived in union with him in our earthly lives, by doing his will."[47] Hope "then is not simply directed to the future, it has immediate moral consequences for the present life."[48] It casts a moral horizon that "transcends a short-sightedness limited to earthly realities."[49]

If there is one form of theological discourse that reminds of the "not yet" while at the same time inspiring hope, it is the slave songs and Black spirituals in American history. These multi-layered modern psalms with titles such as, "Keep Your Eyes on the Prize," "Balm of Gideon," "Steal Away Jesus," "Go Down Moses," and "Ain't Gonna Let Nobody Turn Me Around," proclaimed the possibilities of the future for African Americans during the terrible days of slavery and Jim Crow.[50] They gave hope. Massingale comments on this. "Hope," he writes, "is a stance that good ultimately—but not always—triumphs over evil. . . . Authentic hope is neither illusory nor escapist. It looks squarely at the intransigence of evil . . . yet refuses to accept that evil, tragedy, and defeat will have the final say in human affairs."[51] As Zechariah prays in the Gospel of Luke, "In the tender compassion of our God, the dawn from on high shall break upon us, to shine on those who dwell in darkness and the shadow of death, and to guide our feet into the way of peace" (Luke 1:78–79).

Final Words on the Structure of Moral Theology

Theology (understanding God), anthropology (understanding what it means to be persons), morality (the expectations of behavior and character), and appropriation (living and applying the morality in concrete reality) are the integral elements of moral theology. Moral theology ultimately looks to God, known primarily through Jesus, as its source. It holds a distinctive view of persons informed by this theology. Morality flows from this theologically informed anthropology. Responsible persons then seek to live out this morality in their lives.

A simple takeaway point from the reflection on the kingdom of God is that morality is not about isolated and disconnected individuals. It is not simply about you being a "good" person. Your being a good person is at the same time appropriating and actualizing the kingdom of God in your particular moment and context. Being a good person shrinks the time and space between the "already" and the "not yet." Think about this. You know this is true from your experience of good people and of goodness itself. Life seems to, at least for a time in that space, make sense. Love rolls over and through relationships as the "not yet" invades the present.

Who Was a Neighbor?

The main point of this chapter has been the "structure" of moral theology. The above paragraphs used the theological language from *Gaudium et Spes* to illustrate the "flow-chart" method to discuss the "structure." From there, the basic relationality of life was discussed. The next section will illustrate the "peel-away" method to describe the "structure" of moral theology and it will do so with a very different form of moral discourse. The excerpt from *Gaudium et Spes* was a theological text that used biblical citations and quotes to support its argument. In the next section, we will quote a biblical story and then reflect on its application and meaning.

Luke 10:25–42 contains three distinct but related stories. In the first story, a lawyer challenges Jesus on the interpretation of the Jewish law. In the second story, Jesus himself tells a story, what we all call the parable of the Good Samaritan, to respond to the lawyer. Immediately following this incident, Luke tells the story of Jesus visiting his friends, Mary and Martha, in their home.

I take it that this set of stories illustrates core elements of Jesus' teaching and thus they give us a sense of the foundational elements of Christian life. The genius of Jesus' teaching method here is his use of narrative. Narratives, stories, have an impact on the listener that simple rule giving or abstract philosophical language does not. Good narratives draw the listener into the story and invite the listener to participate. Ultimately, the listener considers what his response would be. We begin with the three stories and then move to some reflection on them leading to the question of inheriting eternal life.

> Just then a lawyer stood up to test Jesus. "Teacher," he said, "what must I do to inherit eternal life?" He said to him, "What is written in the law? What do you read there?" He answered, "You shall love the Lord your God with all your heart, and with all your soul, and with all your strength, and with all your mind; and your neighbor as yourself." And he said to him, "You have given the right answer; do this, and you will live."

> But wanting to justify himself, he asked Jesus, "And who is my neighbor?" Jesus replied, "A man was going down from Jerusalem to Jericho, and fell into the hands of robbers, who stripped him, beat him, and went away, leaving him half dead. Now by chance a priest was going down that road; and when he saw him, he passed by on the other side. So likewise a Levite, when he came to the place and saw him, passed by on the other side. But a Samaritan while traveling came near him; and when he saw him, he was moved with pity. He went to him and bandaged his wounds, having poured oil and wine on them. Then he put him on his own animal, brought him to an inn, and took care of him. The next day he took out two denarii, gave them to the innkeeper, and said, 'Take care of him; and when I come back, I will repay you whatever more you spend.' Which of these

three, do you think, was a neighbor to the man who fell into the hands of the robbers?" He said, "The one who showed him mercy." Jesus said to him, "Go and do likewise."

Now as they went on their way, he entered a certain village, where a woman named Martha welcomed him into her home. She had a sister named Mary, who sat at the Lord's feet and listened to what he was saying. But Martha was distracted by her many tasks; so she came to him and asked, "Lord, do you not care that my sister has left me to do all the work by myself? Tell her then to help me." But the Lord answered her, "Martha, Martha, you are worried and distracted by many things; there is need of only one thing. Mary has chosen the better part, which will not be taken away from her."

On the Samaritan Story

The narrative begins with a lawyer, an expert in religious law, challenging Jesus. He asks Jesus a question to which he already knows the answer. Jesus, however, turns the questioning around and ends up forcing the lawyer to answer a question. The lawyer responds and Jesus affirms his answer. Things are not going as planned for the lawyer. Now he is on trial and not Jesus! Not able to trick Jesus or push him into a corner, the lawyer asks another question. This question demands a definition as an answer, which he could use to judge Jesus. Jesus, again, does not respond the way the lawyer wants. Instead of a definition, Jesus tells a story.

A man is beaten up and left "half dead." Two people, a priest and a Levite, pass by the man. Two other people, a Samaritan and an innkeeper, help the man. In this simple story there are interesting surprises. The first concerns the two people who choose the "lesser part." One was a member of "highest religious leadership" in the community and the other was his "lay associate."[52] The religious leaders ignored the man in need. Commentators have given several reasons for this. They often suggest that the priest and Levite were unable to care for the man because if they touched him, they would

then become ritually impure and that would affect their ability to
serve in the Temple.[53] Scripture says if they touched a dead man they
would be impure for a week (Num. 12:11). If this is the case, then
the "moral" of the story is clear: care for another is more important
than legalism and indeed worship is without meaning if one does
not love others. The priest and Levite were more concerned with ful-
filling their "religious" responsibilities than caring for the needs of a
suffering person.

The second surprise in this story is that those who choose the
"better part" were themselves thought to be morally problematic. It
is not unusual for Old Testament texts to refer to "priests, Levites and
all the people (or children) of Israel" to describe ancient Judaism.[54]
Jesus' audience might very well have expected him to mention an
average person, that is to say, "a child of Israel" in the story after he
talked about the priest and the Levite. Indeed the audience might
have been waiting for an average person to be the hero of the story.
There are places in the New Testament where Jesus is critical of the
religious professionals for their hypocrisy. But that is not how this
story goes. The hero is not a priest or a Levite or an ordinary person.
The hero is a Samaritan.

There were deep ethnic and religious tensions between the Jews
and the Samaritans. A Samaritan would never be a hero in the Jewish
community. Yet for Jesus, the Samaritan chooses the "better part."
Recall the lawyer's initial question: "What must I do to inherit eternal
life?" In the parable the person doing the thing required to inherit
eternal life was not Jewish (and we must add, he was not "Christian")! Jesus seems to be wiping out the usual categories of "who is in
and who is out" regarding eternal life.

Adding to the irony, the Samaritan makes a deal, a partnership of care, with another morally suspect person, an innkeeper. In
Jesus' time, innkeepers did not have a good reputation.[55] The stereo-
type was that they were dishonest and prone to violence. Again an
unlikely character is the moral hero. So we have a "despised half-
breed," the Samaritan, and a person usually thought not to be trust-
worthy, the innkeeper, who give us a "momentary glimpse of the
embodied reign of God."[56]

Jesus' response to the question, "Who is my neighbor?" is central for the Christian life. The neighbor is the next person in need you meet. In other words, everyone is your neighbor. The status of persons as neighbors does not depend on our perception of them as such. They are, regardless of my acknowledgement of them, my neighbors.

Writing in a nontheological context, the contemporary philosopher Amartya Sen comments on this parable as he develops a theory of justice.

> The Samaritan is linked to the wounded Israelite through the event itself: he found the stricken man, saw the need to help, provided that help and was now in a relationship with the injured person. It does not matter whether the Samaritan was moved by charity, or by a "sense of justice," or by some deeper "sense of fairness in treating others as equals." Once he finds himself in this situation, he is in a new "neighborhood."[57]

Sen continues describing the many ways "neighborhoods" are constructed in the contemporary world. He concludes, "There are very few non-neighbors left in the world today."[58] He is correct.

Yet there is more. A second implication for this story is that even though every other person is my neighbor, I must choose to "be" a neighbor to him or to her. Recall the story. After telling the parable, Jesus once again turns the question back onto the lawyer and asks him, "Which of these three, do you think, was a neighbor to the man who fell into the hands of the robbers?" The new question is not, "Who is my neighbor?" It is now, *"Who was a neighbor to the other?"* At the end of the parable our focus is not on the suffering man, but on the Samaritan. Note how the lawyer answers Jesus' question here. He "cannot bring himself to say 'Samaritan'"[59] for he believes the Samaritan is beneath him, so he says instead, "The one who showed him mercy."

Being a neighbor to another demands that I respond to this person in his or her uniqueness and individuality. The man beaten up and left for dead had certain fundamental needs to which the Good Samaritan responded. Jesus says that we are to "Go and do likewise."

On Jesus and the Sisters

Like the parable of the Good Samaritan, the story of Jesus and the Sisters is simple and yet surprising. The first surprise is that Jesus, a single man, visits the women, who are also unmarried, in their home. There is no "chaperone" or other man mentioned in the text.

A second surprise, at least to modern readers, is that Jesus had friends. For some people, the fact that Jesus had friends, that is to say he loved some people in particular and special ways, is problematic. Isn't Jesus supposed to love everybody equally?

The love shown by "Good Samaritans" is as inspiring as it is necessary. But we should not dismiss the significance of loving those "close" to us. Indeed loving family and friends can be more demanding and more intense than loving neighbors. "Friends and family can require degrees of trust, patience and readiness to forgive that go far beyond what is entailed in good will for strangers and enemies."[60] "Indeed, because of the emotional intensity and degrees of vulnerability it involves, love of intimates can be more painful, require many kinds of self-denial, and call upon emotional resources that will not characterize expectations generated from more distant relations."[61] The affirmation that Jesus had friends and that on several occasions his friends betrayed him or let him down ought not be forgotten. How can we love those who we do not know if we cannot love those who we do know?

Another surprise in this story is that Luke describes Mary "sitting at the feet" of Jesus. As many commentators have suggested, this means that Jesus was teaching Mary. She was like his disciple. Yet in Jesus' time, "No self-respecting rabbi could or would endure teaching a woman."[62] Complementing the parable of the Good Samaritan, we have Jesus presenting a new view of who counts in his ministry.

A fourth surprise comes when Martha complains to Jesus about Mary. Martha worked to serve Jesus while Mary merely sat "listening to" Jesus. While the Samaritan is praised as a hero just a few paragraphs above for serving another, it is Mary now who has chosen the "better part" in contrast to Martha who is serving Jesus. Why? Because Martha is "worried and distracted."

The message one gets from the parable of the Good Samaritan seems to contradict Jesus' words to the two women. The parable states that the way to follow Jesus is through work for others while the story of the visit with the two women states that the way to follow Jesus is through sitting down and spending time with him. Yet given the context of the three stories, this does not seem to be an either/or question.

In response to Jesus' question, the lawyer cites two laws from the Old Testament. The first is Deuteronomy 6:5, "You shall love the Lord your God with all your heart, and with all your soul, and with all your strength, and with all your mind." The second is Leviticus 19:18, "You shall love your neighbor as yourself." He presents them together as the basic requirement of the spiritual life. Jesus affirms his answer. There is one "great" commandment and it has two parts. The parable of the Good Samaritan can be read as a reflection on "love your neighbor," and the story of Mary and Martha can be read as a reflection on "love your God." To love God with your whole heart and to love your neighbor as yourself demands both "doing" the word of God and "hearing" the word of God.[63] Together these stories suggest the complementarity and inseparability of contemplation (the internal) and action (the external).

Back to the Lawyer's Question

We began with the text, "Just then a lawyer stood up to test Jesus. 'Teacher,' he said, 'what must I do to inherit eternal life?'" The answer to the question is to love God, others, and oneself. The lawyer's question is interesting not only because of the answer, but how it is worded. The lawyer wants to know *what he can do to get a gift.* Yet a gift is something freely given. An inheritance is something one receives from another, based on a particular relationship one has with the other. But the fulfillment of an inheritance always rests on the giver. The lawyer must know this; indeed there are stories in the Hebrew Scriptures where a "rightful" heir did not receive inheritance (see for example Esau and Jacob, Genesis 25–27). Yet, he wants to do what is within his power to create the conditions to receive the gift of eternal life. And that is to love.

The Good Samaritan story adds something to our understanding about eternal life that perhaps the lawyer was not expecting. Eternal life is not simply something in the future.[64] We can catch glimpses of its beauty here and now. It is "already" present in this world. Look at the Good Samaritan, look at Mary and see a ray of the light that reflects the kingdom of God.

A Readiness to Act

How are we to judge the morality of the main characters in these stories? The priest, the Levite, and Martha seem to get a bad rap. They did nothing wrong. There is no reason to doubt their good intentions or to doubt their virtues. They probably thought they were doing the right thing. Their "guilt" seems to be that they were doing what was generally and ordinarily expected of them. The priest and Levite were supposed to be involved in ritual practice and to do so they had to be ritually pure. Martha was supposed to be doing her household tasks. On any other day, their actions would not be the subject of stories. This day, however, was different.

In both stories we have good people who were unaware of what the particular moment in life demanded. We might say that the three were guilty of not paying attention. In the words of H. Richard Niebuhr, they failed to ask two questions: " 'What is happening?' and then 'What is the fitting response to what is happening?' "[65] They missed something "big"—a suffering neighbor or a chance to have an intimate conversation with Jesus. The priest, the Levite, and Martha did not see the world with the eyes of Jesus. In the words of Pope Francis, "Faith does not merely gaze at Jesus, but sees things as Jesus himself sees them, with his own eyes: it is participation in his way of seeking."[66]

We then see another feature in Jesus' moral teaching—*his implicit challenge for people to examine their hearts*. To his original audience, these stories by and about Jesus are shocking. The Samaritan was the hero; Jesus teaches women; the woman sitting and learning has chosen the "better part" over her busy sister. Imagine if he was telling the Good Samaritan parable to you and someone from a different religion or culture or race or nationality or socio-economic class or sexual orientation (or whatever) was the hero and people you admired in your own "group" were the "priest and Levite?" The people whom you look up to failed and the people whom you look down upon triumphed.

The parable of the Good Samaritan has the obvious takeaway point that you should "Go and do likewise." It also has the deeper shock or surprise element aimed to challenge you to examine your heart. Jesus is telling people something: Practice compassion. The stress is on external teaching and your actions. This addresses a fundamental question of morality, *"What should I do?"* At the same time, he is challenging his listeners to ask themselves a few questions of themselves: I think I am basically a good person, but am I? Why do I think this way about Samaritans (or any other group)? Why do I treat them as I do? The stress is now on internal reflection and discovering your basic commitments, values, dispositions, and character. This addresses a second fundamental question of morality, *"What kind of person am I?"*

The three narratives discussed in this section challenge our view of morality as simply rules or intentions or virtues. The set of expectations are not merely external. Christian morality is about seeing ourselves as persons in relation to and responsive to others. It is about loving, not simply as an action or a goal or a virtue, but as a way we look at the world. In the words of James Gustafson it means to have "readiness to act in certain ways, to seek the interest of others rather than one's own."[67]

The stories remind us that at times our important roles in society need to be put in perspective. We must look up from our duties, limited goals, and self-referring virtues (of being the priest or the Levite or Martha) to love what and how God loves. Christian morality is a response of love to God, our neighbors (close and far) and to ourselves. We must "pay attention" so as not to miss a "half-dead" person or even Jesus as we go about our daily routines and walk on our daily paths. Christian morality, at its best, pushes us so that we will not be like those who asked Jesus, "Lord, when was it that we saw you hungry or thirsty or a stranger or naked or sick in prison, and did not take care of you?" For it pushes us to internalize Jesus' response, "Truly I tell you, just as you did not do it to one of the least of these, you did not do it to me" (Matt. 25:44–45).

Love

There is little doubt that love is at the center of moral theology. We are to love in our daily lives (appropriation) because we are to respond to the love of God (morality) because we are created to love and be loved (anthropology) because God is love and God loves (theology). A short reflection on love and loving is appropriate here.

What Does Love "Look" Like?

St. Augustine (d. 430) and St. Thomas Aquinas (d. 1274) described love as having three elements.[68] The first is the person who loves, the lover. Thomas called this the subject of love. The second is the person or thing loved, the object of love or the beloved. Finally, there is the nature of the love between the lover and the loved. Love has particular features and the appropriate intensity of these features are defined by the relationship between the lover and the loved.

What are we to love? Edward Vacek's thoughts are helpful here. He writes, "A Christian loves, within limits, *what God loves*. What then does God love? In brief, God loves God, the world, other persons, and me. Within our limits, what then should we love? The answer is the same: God, the world, other human beings, and myself. . . . This is not a matter of God first, after that others, and then perhaps oneself. God asks our whole heart all the time, and our love for creatures should increasingly be part of the way we cooperate with God."[69]

But what ought our love "look" like? Within the broader context of the Bible and tradition, we can say a Christian ought to love, within the human condition, *as God loves* or more appropriately, how we experience God. One could use many terms here. For simplicity and clarity, we can say that God's love has five basic characteristics, or better put, our experience of God's love is felt in five ways. It is affective (with emotions), affirming, responsive, unifying, and steadfast. As God loves, we ought to love.[70] This next section considers these five characteristics of God's love.

Love is emotion: For early and medieval Christian theologians, love is the basic human emotion and the source of other emotions.[71] We can think of this emotion as that which moves the "heart" toward something or someone perceived to be good. Love primarily then is an emotion. Indeed most people would describe love as a "strong feeling of affection for another." There are many texts in the Bible that illustrate affective love. Let us look at one powerful example.

The Gospel of John tells a second story about Mary and Martha. In this story we read that their brother Lazarus becomes deathly ill. Mary and Martha send Jesus, who is off in another town, the following message: "Lord, he whom you love is ill" (11:3). John notes that Jesus loved the women and their brother (11:5). For some reason, he says, Jesus takes his time getting to his friends; indeed he arrives four days after Lazarus's death. When Jesus meets up with the women, Mary is weeping. John writes: "When Jesus saw her weeping . . . he was greatly disturbed in spirit and deeply moved. He said, 'Where have you laid him?' They said to him, 'Lord, come and see. Jesus began to weep. So the Jews said, 'See how he loved him!' " (11:33–36).

This is a remarkable line. Jesus wept over the death of his friend. One cannot help but to cry over the loss of a loved one. Affections and emotions are critical elements of loving. Love produces emotions: joy or laughter or smiles or twinkles of the eye or feeling good or even sadness or pain. You cannot love without "feeling" it. I am not saying here that God is emotional. I am saying that we experience God's love with some emotion.

The opposite of love in this sense is not hate. The opposite of love in this sense is not being moved by what one knows to be good. It is when one has no affection or emotion. It is saying, "I really do not care about you." The opposite of love in this sense is apathy or indifference.

Love responds: Yet love is more than an emotion. As we have seen in Luke 10, love includes some response to the one loved. When one loves, the beloved is never an object or a thing. He or she is always a person. This person is a unique and beautiful individual with basic human needs and desires. Love is a reply or a reaction to the other. Words such as "care" or "mercy" or "concern" express the responsiveness of love. The opposite of responsiveness is ignoring the other's needs, wants, and dreams while putting our own needs, wants, and dreams first.

In Exodus, God hears the cries of the oppressed and works to deliver them (Exod. 2–3). In Hosea, God is said to take the people up in his arms and heal them (Hos. 11:3). The Gospel of John states, "For God so loved the world that he gave his only Son" (John 3:16). Jesus tells Peter that if he loves him, he ought to "feed my sheep" (John 21:15–17). Jesus himself feeds, heals, and teaches countless people. Paul's famous description of love is written in responsive language: "Love is patient, kind; it is not envious or boastful or arrogant or rude. It does not insist on its own way; it is not irritable or resentful; it does not rejoice in wrongdoing, but rejoices in the truth" (1 Cor 13:4–6). We are to love, we are told in 1 John, not merely in "word or speech, but in truth and action" (1 John 3:18).

Ultimately, one responds to the other with oneself. Taking care of the needs of the other is good and true but the deeper love is giving of the self to the other. Pope Benedict XVI's encyclical *Deus Caritas Est* (God is love) describes this feature well. Love, he writes, is a "journey, an ongoing exodus out of the closed inward-looking self toward its liberation through self-giving." Benedict continues, "My deep personal sharing in the needs and sufferings of others becomes a sharing of my very self with them: if my gift is not to prove a source of humiliation, I must give to others not only something that is my own, but my very self; I must be personally present in my gift."[72]

Theologian Jules Toner describes it this way: "For the giving which is love is not merely a giving to someone for the other to possess and use. . . . It is giving self. For it is myself who am in the loved one by my love, not merely my possession, or even my thoughts, my wit, my joy my wisdom, my strength. It is myself."[73] In love I meet the vulnerable other with my vulnerability. Vulnerability is crucial for good relationships and good relationships provide the conditions for protecting our vulnerability.

I suspect that for many people the path to mature responsive love begins with and constantly depends on a basic love of self. This love, if honest, grows into loving others. Equally important here is that basic love of self is part of being open to being loved by others. Indeed, no one can be said to be loving if he or she cannot accept love from others.

The notion of self-love deserves significant reflection in theology. Experience shows us at least three things. First, we all know people who "love" themselves a bit too much. They are self-centered, egotistical, and selfish. It is hard to be good friends with these sorts of people because they are not responsive to you as a person. On the other hand, we all know people who lack an appropriate love for themselves. We experience them as immature, pessimistic, negative, dependent, and lacking basic self-confidence. On the extreme end of this, these people can be self-destructive. People who lack basic self-love often have problems responding to you in friendship. When we talk about basic self-love, we are talking about something in the middle. This is a fundamental, positive, healthy love for oneself.

Let's return for a moment to Pope Benedict's reflections on love. Benedict thinks about love from within a tradition that holds there are the stages in love. Love "begins" with the natural love of self.[74] Love grows as it discovers the reality of another person and matures to the level of "concern and care for the other."[75] Self-seeking love, he writes, now developed into love for another, "is ready, and even willing, for sacrifice."[76] This is, of course, the story of the Good Samaritan. This is also implicit in the Great Commandment, for we are to love our neighbor *as* ourselves. The "as" can indicate "like" or "in the same way that."

When St. Augustine reflected on the Great Commandment, he noted, "It is clear that love for yourself is not omitted."[77] He wrote, "You should love yourself not only on your own account but on account of Him who is most justly the object of your love."[78] "For," he continues, "it is impossible for one who loves God not to love himself."[79] Or, "He who knows how to love himself loves God."[80] Appropriate self-love is so important for Augustine and he says we must love ourselves more than we love others. "There are four kinds of things which may be loved—first, the kind which is above us; second, the kind which constitutes ourselves; third, the kind which is equal to us; and fourth, the kind which is below us—no precepts need to be given concerning the second and the fourth. However much a man departs from the truth, there remains in him the love of himself and of his body."[81]

The writings of St. Bernard of Clairvaux (d. 1113) are helpful here. Bernard wrote at great length about loving God. We come to mature love for God, he says, through four stages, or in his words, "degrees." Each stage builds on the other. Much of what he says about loving God can be related to loving other people.

Bernard's first two steps are self-centered. They are necessary to advance in love, but if one stays at the particular step, one's love is not developed; it is immature. The first step is to love oneself for one's own sake. The second is to love God for one's own sake. We all begin relationships with a basic love for ourselves. When we first form relationships with others, we usually do so because we "get something" out of the relationships.

But according to Bernard, there are more stages. Here is what he says about the person who is at this stage. "When forced by his own needs he begins to honor God and care for him by thinking of him, reading about him, praying to him, and obeying him. God reveals himself gradually in this kind of familiarity and consequently becomes lovable. When man tastes how sweet God is, he passes to the third degree of love in which man loves God not now because of himself but because of God."[82] The fourth degree, says Bernard, is when one comes to love oneself for the sake of God.

The third stage is easy to relate to maturing love among persons. After a time of being with another, sharing with another, and experiences of mutual vulnerability and caring, one comes to love the other for who the other is and not for what one can get out of the relationship. All of this starts on and depends on basic love for self.

Edward Vacek writes, "God passionately wants our good."[83] Vacek draws our attention to two extremes, one of too much self-giving and the other of too much self-concern. "Other-centered and self-sacrificial agape is essential in the Christian's heart. There are roughly equivalent dangers of excessive self-assertion and self-giving. The danger of self-love is selfishness. The danger of other-love is that we treat ourselves merely as *means* for the fulfillment of the interests of others."[84]

In response, Vacek recalls the three Greek words associated with love, namely, *agape, eros* and *philia*. He then defines these classic words in relation to the basic intentions of the lover. Thus *agape* is love "for the sake of the beloved"; *eros* is love "for our own sake;" *How People Talk about Morality* and *philia* is love "for the sake of a relationship" I have with another. [85] *Philia*, he argues, "is the most complete Christian love."[86] Indeed it "is the foundation and goal of Christian life . . . all human love finds its culmination and ultimate goal in a community of solidarity with and in God."[87]

When one loves God as God loves, *agape, eros,* and *philia* balance each other. *Agape* corrects selfishness and pride, as well as our tendencies to exclusiveness. In times of depression or self-hate, *eros* enlivens us to goodness and indeed to our own goodness, potentially making us able to love others more. "*Philia*," Vacek writes, "corrects the temptation to think that life is nothing more than individuals walking next to, or behind or in front of others, but not with others."[88]

Appropriate, or in more traditional language "ordered," self-love is self-love understood within the context of a God who loves us and our attempts to love this loving God. "My full love occurs when *I* love *my* God."[89]

The above paragraphs argued that a basic love of self is necessary to loving respond to others. There are other things to say about response in love, indeed the lawyer's question to Jesus seems to capture them all: "Who is my neighbor?" To whom am I to respond in love? Perhaps, like the Good Samaritan, we must respond in love to others who are "close" to us before we are able to respond in love those who are "far" from us. We love family, friends, and so on before we can love strangers. Some theologians rightly warn us of the moral limitations of loving only the easy people to love. They call this "safe" neighbor love. We must not allow our justified love for those "close" to us to be an excuse not to love those who are "far" from us.[90]

Love for those "close" to us, again if honest, ought to grow into loving those "far" from us. There are people who are *literally* "far" from us, for example, people separated from us by time and distance. There are also people *metaphorically* "far" from us, for example people of different races or cultures or social status who may indeed not be literally "far" from us. If we are able to love God and those "far" from us, we then revise our love for ourselves and for those close to us.[91]

Love affirms: If the emotion of love leads to a response to the other, the response of love always affirms the other for who he or she is as a person. To "affirm" someone is to say "yes" to him or her. Loving confirms the truthfulness of the other as a person.

Again there are many examples of this aspect of love in the Bible. The famous story where the scribes and Pharisees (the religious leaders of Jesus' time) bring a woman caught in adultery to Jesus stands out. The law commanded them to kill the woman by throwing stones at her. The leaders challenged Jesus on this and questioned him on what they should do. Jesus said, "Let anyone among you who is without sin be the first to throw a stone at her" (John 8:7). No one did; indeed they all left the scene. Jesus, in words of love, said to the woman, "Go your way, and from now on do not sin again" (John 8:11). One would think that she left at once challenged to change yet affirmed as a person.

The opposite of affirmation is all-too-easy to see in daily life. It is seen in acts that belittle or that put others down. It is seen in oppression and domination. The feeling of being used or being humiliated is the opposite of the feeling of being affirmed.

Love unites: Affective, responsive, and affirming love necessarily leads to some sense of unity. Love always unites. The unity of love is frequently found in Scripture. In the Old Testament we read Ruth's famous words of love to Naomi, "Where you go, I will go; where you lodge, I will lodge; your people shall be my people, and your God my God. Where you die, I will die—there will I be buried" (Ruth 1:16–17). Twice in Song of Solomon, the famous love poem, we hear one of the voices say, "My beloved is mine and I am his" (Song of Solomon 2:16, 6:3). Several of Jesus' parables have the unitive feature of love as a theme. In the Prodigal Son, Jesus tells the story of the father seeing his sinful son returning home. Luke writes, "But while he was still far off, his father saw him and was filled with compassion; he ran and put his arms around him and kissed him" (Luke 15:20).

Love is relational and unitive in all its expressions. As Benedict says, we must receive the gift of love from others even as we give our love to others.[92] Full love in his view is union, union with God, union with particular others, union in community, and unity in humanity. "But," as Benedict notes, "this union is no mere fusion, a sinking in the nameless ocean of the Divine; it is a unity which creates love, a unity in which both God and man remain themselves and yet become fully one."[93] Love "is a force that builds community, it brings all people together without imposing barriers or limits. The unity of the human race, a fraternal communion transcending every barrier, is called into being by the word of God-who-is-Love."[94]

Love fails with discord and violence. It withers with divisiveness and conflict. This can be intentional or maybe unintentional as when people say they have "drifted" or "grown" apart. The level of unity, of course, depends on the type of relationship and the expectations of the relationship.

Love endures: Finally, as an affective affirmation that is responsive and unitive, love is not and cannot be fleeting. Love is lasting. It is faithful, steadfast, and enduring. This certainly is a characteristic of God's love. Psalm 136 illustrates this quite poetically. It begins, "O give thanks to the LORD, for he is good, for his steadfast love endures forever." That verse is followed by twenty-four verses, each ending with the phrase, "his steadfast love endures forever." The psalm ends, "O give thanks to the God of heaven, for his steadfast love endures forever."

St. Paul writes of the enduring aspect of love on several occasions. In his Letter to the Romans he states, "I am convinced that neither death, nor life, nor angels, nor rules, nor things present, nor things to come, nor powers, nor height, nor depth, nor anything else in all creation, will be able to separate us from the love of God in Christ Jesus our Lord" (Rom. 8:38–39). Paul proclaims that love "bears all things, believes all things, hope all things, endures all things. Love never ends. . . . And now faith, hope, and love abide, these three; and the greatest of these is love" (1 Cor. 13:7–8, 13).

Enduring does not mean unchanging. People grow in love. The point of moral development and moral maturity is to become more able to love *what* God loves and *how* God loves. We do so within our situated freedom, to love what God loves in the way that God loves.

Justice: The "Eyes" of Love

The greatest commandment (or rule) in Christian life is twofold: To love God with your whole self and to love your neighbor as yourself.

The New Testament is dramatically clear about this.[95] But love is not simply a rule here. It is also a fundamental intention and goal we ought to have in life. The Gospel of Luke, for example, tells a story of Jesus eating with the Pharisees. During the meal a woman whom Luke describes as a "sinner" crashes the party and makes a scene. She stands behind Jesus and cries. She then washes Jesus' feet with her tears and dries them with her hair. There is more. She kisses his feet and anoints them with oil! The Pharisees are shocked. According to Luke, Jesus tells a parable and then pronounces forgiveness on the woman. He forgives her because "she has shown great love" (Luke 7:47).

This story is often used to show Jesus' power to forgive. This seems to miss the point. The story, at least according to Jesus, is about the power of this woman's love. If she, a sinner, is able to show such great love, so ought we. We see that love was more than a rule for the woman. It was her goal, her end, reflecting her fundamental intention in the act.

In the New Testament, love is a command and an expected intention or goal in life. The stories of the Good Samaritan and Mary and Martha indicate that love, the affective affirmation that is responsive, unitive, and enduring, is also a character trait. It is a virtue, a "habit of the heart and mind." In Christian morality then, love is a basic expectation for our behavior as well as our character. Our flourishing depends on our loving and indeed on the love of others.

There is, however, more to morality than love. Love often needs direction and focus, particularly for those of us who have not yet perfected it (that would be all of us!). Let's use another metaphor to describe a second essential feature of Christian morality. "Seeing" has been a metaphor for interpreting, discerning, and understanding since at least Plato's famous allegory of the cave. If love then is the "heart" of morality, justice serves as the "eyes" of morality. Justice helps us to "see" the what, when, where, why, and how of love. It directs the day-to-day living of love.

Like love, justice is a fundamental theme of biblical morality.[96] Like love, justice is a rule or expectation for our actions. It is also a goal and a virtue. *Love informed by justice* ought then to be the fundamental approach to our being in the world.

In the Bible, justice is presented as a behavioral expectation, that is to say, as a rule or a required intention/goal. Consider the following quotations. Psalm 106:4, "Happy are those who observe justice." Psalms 10:18 and 82:3–4, "Do justice for the orphan and the oppressed," and "Give justice to the weak and the orphan; maintain the right of the lowly and the destitute." Isaiah 1:17, "Seek justice, rescue the oppressed, defend the orphan, plead for the widow." Jeremiah 22:3, "Thus says the LORD: Act with justice and righteousness, and deliver from the hand of the oppressor anyone who has been robbed." Amos 5:15, 24, "Establish justice" and "Let justice roll down like waters and righteous like and ever-flowing stream." Finally the often-quoted lines of Micah 6:8, "He has told you, O mortal, what is good; and what does the Lord require of you but to do justice, and to love kindness; and to walk humbly with your God?"

Thomas Aquinas's medieval description of justice is perhaps the best virtue-based definition of justice we have. In his words, "Justice is the habit whereby a person renders to each one his or her due by a constant and perpetual will."[97] We have already discussed the notion of moral habit. Justice then is the habit of the heart and mind where one gives, constantly and always, to each person what is due to them. The definition seems straightforward; the only ambiguous thing here is what exactly is *due* to another?

Moral theology offers the following indicators of justice, that is to say, what is due to another. Put simply, people are due things based on *two basic sets of relationships* in proportionate response to *three moral norms*. The primary relationship is membership in the human family. Persons by their nature as persons are due basic things from other persons based on the common human nature. These basic things are the conditions needed for the possibility of flourishing. These minimal conditions are called human rights (see the list of human rights in chapter 2 from Pope John XXIII's encyclical *Pacem in Terris)*.

Second, persons are due certain things based on their particular relationship to you. As we said earlier, you are a brother or sister, son or daughter, friend, neighbor, husband or wife, cousin, citizen of a city, county, state and nation. You are a member of various groups: for example, clubs or a church, a team or political party or professional association. Moral claims and expectations arise from within those relationships. You "owe" things to your children that you do not "owe" to the children who live across the street from you. You "owe" things to your spouse that you do not "owe" to the parents of the children who live across the street from you.

Along with these two basic sets of relationships are three moral norms. Like most views of justice, moral theology highlights the proportionate relationship, or creative tension, between "justice as fairness" and "justice as equality." Equality means that everyone is due the same good or the same amount of the good. For example, we have equal liberties and we all have equal votes in an election (one!). Fairness is an appropriate unequal distribution of goods based on a publicly justified and reasonable standard. It is fair that a CEO of a company gets paid more than the person who sweeps the floors of the company. This is not to say that there are no reasonable limits to the unequal pay.

The best example of equality and fairness I can think of is in my role as a teacher. In justice, I am morally obligated to treat all my students equally. I cannot favor one over the other. It would be immoral of me to be biased or to discriminate against some of them. But at the same time I am morally obligated to grade my students fairly, which may indeed mean unequally. In any course, students earn various grades. It would be immoral for me to give them all the same grade if they all performed differently on exams, papers, and more.

Above we had a selection of quotations from the Bible on justice. While these quotations may have included the implicit sense of fairness and equality, they all expressed the explicit expectation that justice includes direct action to care for the vulnerable. In the words of the Pontifical Biblical Commission, "the privileged concern for the poor" is a "structural and essential" element in biblical morality. "This theme," they write, "is to be found from one end of Scripture to the other." Thus justice fully understood by Christians is truly justice when the needs of the orphan, the oppressed, the weak, the lowly, the destitute, and the widow are addressed. Thus the triangle for justice in moral theology: equality, fairness, and a directive focus on the needs of the vulnerable.

Justice, understood through the two sets of relationships and the three norms, serves as the "eyes" for the "heart" of love. Lived out, justice is the moral bond of relationships as it aims to set up the possibilities for persons to flourish.

Morally mature Christians must come to grips with the expansive and radical love of God. They do this through particular loves that are affective, responsive, affirming, uniting, and steadfast. If these loves are true, they necessarily open them up to loving "Samaritans" and others. Recognizing others as persons and living out the created relationality between persons, morally mature Christians redefine their "neighborhood" and, with it, themselves. There is no deeper expression of the "theology" in moral theology.

Moral Identity

Moral identity is primarily an internal question. The discussion of the structure of moral theology in this chapter, on the other hand, seems very external. Theology and anthropology are abstract ideas "up there" in the clouds. Yet, there is a relationship. Your moral identity is directly related to your sense of what grounds your moral views. Asking the questions, "What is your theology?" or "What is your anthropology?" may seem academic, but they are real. Another way of saying this is "What do you stand for?" or "What do you really believe or hold dear to your heart?" More often than not, your actions are illustrations of your answers to these questions.

A basic teaching of moral theology is that one's moral identity ought to be formed on love and justice. Fundamental to your flourishing and your moral identity is the ability to love and to accept love. Justice, as the "eyes of love," helps us to live out 1 John's maxim, "Let us love, not in word or speech, but in truth and action" (1 John 3:18). One's moral identity ought to include a determined sense of service to others and a space for a sense of reflection in your life.

Questions

1. If the description of love in this chapter is correct, then the characteristics described should relate to all types of loving relationships (including intimate love, friendship, relationships within families, and even friendships based on work or common activities). Yet, how do these characteristics differ in various types of relationships?

2. Discuss the opposite of each of the characteristics of love and how each creates an impediment to friendship or intimate love.

3. Discuss the development of friendships or intimate relationships and how each of the characteristics of love grows and changes as the relationship develops.

4. Discuss how the kingdom of God might apply to contemporary moral thinking.

5. Discuss the Pontifical Biblical Commission's reflections on the six features of morality.

6. Discuss how and why the author uses the Bible in this chapter (note the sources the author relies on). What might be different or alternative ways of using the Bible in this context? What is your response to the use of the Bible in this chapter?

CHAPTER FOUR

Actions and Persons

For every thing there is a season,
and a time for every matter under heaven:
a time to be born, and a time to die;
a time to plant, and a time to pluck up what is planted;
a time to kill, and a time to heal;
a time to break down, and a time to build up;
a time to weep, and a time to laugh;
a time to mourn, and a time to dance;
a time to throw away stones, and a time to gather stones together;
a time to embrace, and a time to refrain from embracing;
a time to seek, and a time to lose;
a time to keep, and a time to throw away;
a time to tear, and a time to sew;
a time to keep silence, and a time to speak;
a time to love, and a time to hate;
a time for war, and a time for peace.   —Ecclesiastes 3:1–8

The morality of the human act depends primarily and fundamen-
tally on the "object" rationally chosen by the deliberate will. . . . In
order to be able to grasp the object of an act which specifies that act
morally, it is therefore necessary to place oneself in the perspective
of the acting person. The object of the act of willing is in fact a freely
chosen kind of behavior. . . . By the object of a given moral act, then,
one cannot mean a process or an event of the merely physical order,
to be assessed on the basis of its ability to bring about a given state
of affairs in the outside world. Rather, that object is the proximate
end of a deliberate decision which determines the act of willing on
the part of the acting person.   —John Paul II, *Veritatis Splendor*

These opening quotations express the general problems considered in this chapter. The first is a poem from the book Ecclesiastes in the Old Testament. The poem highlights the nature of human action. In short, we act in contexts we do not construct ourselves: "There is a time to plant and a time to pluck what is planted." The second is from Pope John Paul II's encyclical *Veritatis Splendor*. The quote invites us to reflect on human action as a product of choice, purpose, and freedom. This chapter begins with three narratives used to illustrate the elements of moral reflection on particular actions. It then moves to the question of whether some actions are always wrong and the related question of sin. Surrounding these questions is the issue of the fullness of one's life narrative.

The Morality of Acts

Let's say that you had a hectic day at work. You return home tired, hungry, and a bit irritable. As you walk in the door, your roommate says something simple and seemingly harmless to you. Her words, however, strike you in the wrong way and they "cause" you to snap. You say something in response. The words just fly out of your mouth. You quickly realize that you said something that you should not have said. Now a scene has been created and your roommate says something, something not very nice, back to you. The downward spiral of misunderstanding leads you to a place where you had no intention of going. You brought your bad day home with you!

Think about this incident. It is hard to say what the real cause of the misunderstanding was. There is a whole history of interactions between you and your roommate. But let's focus on this particular incident. You said something that hurt or insulted your friend. In a very real, yet not physical way, you harmed her. You are, however, surprised, because you did not *intend* to hurt her. You try to tell her later that you had not meant to say what you said. She reminds you that you, however, did say that.

How are we to judge your action here? Traditional moral theology suggests a way to consider specific actions. The method is called the "three-font principle." In all morally relevant situations, there are three parts of a person acting: namely, the basic action, the intention, and the circumstances.

First, there is an *action*. Recall our distinction between "simple" or "complex" goods. Within the experience of freedom you choose specific goals. Think of an action then as the means to achieving something, a means to an end, a thing done for some purpose. The "action" is you directing yourself toward a goal or goals in the particular context. In more technical terms, the "action itself" is the object freely chosen by the person.

In this case of you yelling at your roommate, the actions are your words directed at your roommate. This includes your choice of words and your choice of how you delivered the words to your roommate. It is not just the words themselves that matter; it is the attitude, tone, and loudness of the words.

Second, all morally relevant action includes *intentionality*. The intention is the "internal part" of the action. Quoting theologian Richard Gula, the intention "is also called the 'end,' or that which we are after in doing what we do." The intention of any act is critical. According to Gula (and I think he is correct), the intention is the "whole purpose of our action. The intention gives personal meaning to what we do."[2] That is to say, the intention is the "you" in the action.

Finally, every action occurs within a particular set of *circumstances*. Think about the meaning of the word "circumstance." *Circum* is Latin for around. The circumstances of an action then are the conditions around the act, the context in which the act occurred, and, in some ways, the consequences of the action.

According to the three-font principle, we must consider all three elements together to understand the moral meaning of an action. Thus we cannot evaluate an action without knowing the intention of the person acting and the circumstances in which the action occurred. In a textbook, it is easy to break down an action into these three parts. In real life, it seems much harder to do so. Real life is complex. But let's try.

What exactly did you do when you came home and yelled at your roommate? You might say that you were "blowing off steam." You felt like you needed to express yourself and get the day's frustration "out of your system." These seem to be perfectly reasonable things to do. You did not intend to raise your voice at your roommate and you certainly did not want to hurt her feelings. But, of course, you did yell and she was hurt. To quote a character in a Kaye Gibbons novel, "You can't ever just throw words out. They have to land somewhere."[3]

When you try to explain yourself to her, all three of these things come together: your bad day (the circumstances), your quick response to her (your intention), and then, of course, the words and how they were delivered (the action). The way you see it, the circumstances just piled up and you simply responded in the situation. You believe that the *meaning of your act* lies in understanding the circumstances. You had a terrible day and you were simply "blowing off steam." If the circumstances were different, you would not have responded that way. The circumstances and lack of intention to harm, in your mind, gave meaning to the act.

She does not see it that way; and I think she is right. Understanding the circumstances, the "who, what, when, where, why, how, what else, and what if"[4] in an action are critical for the full moral meaning of an act, particularly for considering questions of accountability and responsibility. But in themselves the circumstances can never fully account for the morality of your action and indeed of any action. In the three-font principle, circumstances are important, but they are secondary to the action itself and the intentions.

Actions are the external expressions of one's heart. They exhibit one's character. They are illustrations of what one believes and values. They are also attempts to actualize goals springing from intentions. Actions can be evaluated in relation to rules. A basic human action then relates to three of the four elements of morality. For these reasons, the action itself and the intention "behind" always "count more" than circumstances.

It is hard to imagine a situation where the circumstances would be the primary element in moral reflection. If we give circumstances equal weight in moral reflection with the intention and the action itself, we deny the real harm people can do to others. The "situation" can be inappropriately used to justify all sorts of evils. Thus people have defended slavery on economic circumstances. They have defended social discrimination on cultural situations. People have said that the circumstances of war make the killing of innocent civilians understandable or that they justify torture ("get over it, that's what happens in war"). You tried to justify your yelling on the fact that you had a bad day. But this sort of argument is problematic. Circumstances are essential to the moral evaluation of an act but they are not the primary elements in such evaluation. In the words of the *Catechism*, they are the "secondary elements of a moral act." They can increase or diminish the goodness or evil of an act. They can also increase or diminish a person's responsibility for an act.[5] All of this is to say, you were wrong for yelling at your roommate.

But perhaps I am too hasty in my judgment. You might say that it is one's intention that really matters. Intentions make the action. Think of a different situation. Let's say you and your roommate are in the kitchen cleaning. You are sweeping the floor and she is cleaning the stove. You bend down to pick up something off the floor and the broom slips out of your hand, hitting your roommate on the head. Once again, you hurt her. This time, however, the pain is physical (and she may soon be looking for a new roommate!).

In an important way, this act is different from the yelling incident. You should have been more careful holding the broom, but in the end, gravity won out. It was an accident; the broom slipped out of your hand. The yelling incident was not an accident. Part of the reason that your roommate was hurt is because she knows that you can control your voice. Your vocal cords are not like gravity. At some level you made the choice to say what you said.

Think of yet another situation. You need money and you go into your roommate's purse and take out a twenty-dollar bill without asking her and without telling her about this later. You know you will not repay her. In this story, your intentionality is direct and clear. You wanted the money and you took it from her.

Notice the three levels of intentionality in these stories. Gula is correct when he states, "We cannot judge the morality of the physical action without reference to the meaning of the whole action which includes the intention of the agent."[6] In the kitchen story, we have an accident. There is no "you" in the act of the broom hitting her head. Unless you want to say that "you are clumsy." You did nothing "immoral" as the broom dropped from your hand. In the money story you acted freely and purposively, that is to say, with clear intention. Here you did something "immoral." You took something that was not yours. In the yelling incident, the circumstances influenced your decision to yell and you were not morally strong enough to hold your words back. Your action was immoral, but perhaps not in the same way as was your stealing. You did harm to another person in each of the three situations, yet the level of you "in" each act is different, and thus the moral evaluation of each is different.

So how much "weight" should we give to the person's intention? There is no doubt that intention is crucial. This is why John Paul II declared, "The morality of the human act depends primarily and fundamentally on the 'object' rationally chosen by the deliberate will." In order to really understand the meaning of an act of another person then, he wrote, "it is therefore necessary to place oneself in the perspective of the acting person."[7] This is a very interesting statement. In order to understand another's action, we must come to know what is going on inside the person.

Our extended focus on intentionality here is significant, because it is directly related to accountability. If one intentionally performs an act, one is accountable for that action. That is to say, it is "your" action. You are responsible for that action. But if we "place oneself in the perspective" of another person, and indeed, if we reflect on our own actions, we see that issues of accountability and responsibility may not be as clear as we might think. We are now back to the "secondary elements of the moral act," circumstances. There may be mitigating circumstances that affect responsibility. In the words of the *Catechism*, "Responsibility for an action can be diminished or even nullified by ignorance, inadvertence, duress, fear, habit, inordinate attachments, and other psychological or social factors."[8] Notice all these words. They all refer to lack of freedom from interference. The interference may be external or indeed the interference may be internal.

According to the three-font principle, for an action to be good and appropriate, both the intention and the action itself ought to be good. Put simply, we need these two to be positive for the full act to be good. The "number three" font, circumstances, helps us reflect on the level of moral accountability for both good acts and bad acts. People can do the right thing for wrong reasons and can do harm with good intentions. Ethicist James Keenan writes, "Good people may have right intentions but still fall short in realizing them as right choices."[9] Again, Keenan says, "A right action cannot necessarily deductively indicate a good motivation, nor can a good motivation guarantee the attainment of moral rightness."[10]

An Action and a Life Story

The general objective of this part of the chapter has been to explain and to suggest the usefulness of the three-font principle. The three-font principle helps us understand the moral meaning of an action. Its strength lies in its examination of the totality of an action, that is to say, it considers all the morally relevant factors. I might add that its primary use ought to be by persons reflecting on their own choices, although we tend to use it more frequently to critique the actions of others. While I want to affirm the place of the three-font principle in moral reflection, I also want to note that in a broader sense, it cannot stand alone. The point of the three-font principle is to understand the morality of *an action*. There are many times in our lives (perhaps daily!) when we must come to terms with a particular action. Yet there is more, much more, to the meaning of our moral lives than simply looking at the moral meaning of one particular action. Very rarely does it happen in your life where you can say that one action you have taken defines your whole self. All people, including good people, make moral mistakes. Frankly, we need a four-font principle.

Let's return to the initial story of you and your roommate. Most people would probably say that you should not have yelled at her. That is to say, that it was wrong for you to yell at her. But should our moral reflection stop with that statement? Do you think it is fair to describe you as one who comes home and yells at roommates? There are other things we should consider here. The first is the history and nature of your relationship to your roommate, the second is what you did after the event, and the third concerns the relationship of the act to your overall character. The full moral meaning of the act must be understood in relation to the narrative of your life. So we need to ask more questions. For example, does this happen regularly? Do you lose your temper frequently? Is it "normal" for you take out your frustrations on others? If the answer to these questions seems to be yes, do you see a problem here? Are you mature enough to want to change this behavior?

To put it another way, was this action "in character" for you? Was it an expression of who you are as a person? More specifically: Are you insensitive? Are you temperamental? Notice these words. We have moved from describing a specific act, namely yelling, to describing an enduring feature of your personality. Recall the discussion of the elements of morality in the first chapter: rules, intentions, and virtues. In a sense you broke a rule when you yelled at your roommate. You certainly broke a rule when you stole money from her purse. While there is no moral rule prohibiting yelling, it is generally agreed upon that a primary moral rule is "Do not harm others." Much of the discussion above has addressed the role of intention and goals. We are now thinking about character traits, those enduring features of our personality that influence our behaviors.

An overemphasis on the three-font principle may lead to a judgmental or condescending view of others. Neither you nor I, however, would want others to judge us based on one unfortunate bad action. As we are inclined to judge others, we ought to remember Jesus' engaging image. We must be sure to remove the "log" in our own eye before we remove the "speck" in another's eye (Matt. 7:3).

Christians would do well to recall that two of Jesus' most important apostles, saints Peter and Paul, made huge moral mistakes. St. Peter, the "rock" of the church (and for Catholics, the first pope), denied knowing Jesus three times while Jesus was being beaten ("then they spat in his face and struck him; and some slapped, him" Matt. 26:69–75). St. Paul described his former life to the Galatians as follows: "You have heard, no doubt, of my earlier life in Judaism. I was violently persecuting the church of God and was trying to destroy it" (Gal. 1:13).[11] Denying Jesus and persecuting Christians are important moments in their lives, yet ultimately we judge them not on these particular actions but rather on the full narratives of their lives.

The three-font principle is a helpful tool for moral reflection. Many of our actions are simple and simply good or bad. As we will see in the next chapter, an important feature in developing a good conscience is the practice of self-reflection. We note, however, the limitations of the three-font principle. The full moral meaning of a particular action, good or bad, may take days, weeks, or much longer to process and understand.

Acts That Are Always Wrong

According to the three-font principle, we need to examine the intention of the person acting, the act itself and the circumstances to determine the morality of a particular action. The intention and the act itself must be good in order for the act as a whole to be judged good. This view of the morality of action, however, is not complete. Most people think that some acts by their nature preclude them from being analyzed by the three-font principle. These acts are said to be *intrinsically evil*. That is to say, no intention or circumstances could ever justify them.

The Catholic Church teaches this. Pope John Paul II, for example, offers a list of such actions. He writes,

> Whatever is opposed to life itself, such as any type of murder, genocide, abortion, euthanasia or willful self-destruction, whatever violates the integrity of the human person, such as mutilation, torments inflicted on body or mind, attempts to coerce the will itself; whatever insults human dignity, such as subhuman living conditions, arbitrary imprisonment, deportation, slavery, prostitution, the selling of women and children; as well as disgraceful working conditions, where men are treated as mere tools for profit, rather than as free and responsible persons.[12]

The Second Vatican Council includes on this list "every type of dis-crimination, whether social or cultural, whether based on sex, race, color, social condition, language or religion."[13] John Paul II adds con-traceptive practices to the Council's list.[14] The *Catechism* includes blasphemy, perjury, murder, adultery, masturbation, and homo-sexual acts.[15]

We might add more. For the past several years, Catholics have been thoroughly embarrassed by the actions of some members of the clergy, brothers, priests and bishops, in the sex abuse scandals around the globe. Certainly rape, child abuse, forced sexual activity, as well as steps taken to protect the rapists and abusers (often put-ting other children in harm's way), are all intrinsically evil. No inten-tions or circumstances would morally allow for these, ever.

We could still add more actions to this category. The use of par-ticular weapons in war, weapons that do not distinguish between enemy soldiers and civilians, is intrinsically evil. Indeed the U.S. Catholic Bishops suggest that any use of nuclear weapons is an intrinsic evil.[16] The following paragraph, which is an official sum-mary of the Catholic Church's view of war, seems to state that all war is intrinsically evil:

> The Magisterium condemns "the savagery of war" and asks that war be considered in a new way. In fact, "it is hardly possible to imagine that in an atomic era, war could be used as an instrument of justice." War is a "scourge" and is never an appropriate way to resolve problems that arise between nations, "it has never been and it will never be," because it creates new and still more complicated conflicts. When it erupts, war becomes an "unnecessary massacre," an "adventure without return" that compromises humanity's present and threatens its future. "Nothing is lost by peace; everything may be lost by war." The damage caused by an armed conflict is not only material but also moral. In the end, war is "the failure of all true humanism," "it is always a defeat for humanity;" "never again some peoples against others, never again! . . . no more war, no more war!"[17]

A strong argument can be made that smoking cigarettes is intrinsically evil. According to the American Lung Association, "Smoking harms nearly every organ in the body, and is a main cause of lung cancer and chronic obstructive pulmonary disease (COPD, including chronic bronchitis and emphysema). It is also a cause of coronary heart disease, stroke, and a host of other cancers and diseases."[18] It is hard to imagine any intention that would make smoking a morally good or even a morally neutral act. But this brings up a few interesting points. Before the 1964 U.S. Surgeon General's report, "Smoking and Health," we could not legitimately say that smoking was an intrinsic evil. This says something about true ignorance and culpability (as well as strong cultural and market forces glamorizing actions that ultimately frustrate human flourishing). The judgment of something being intrinsically evil depends on sound reasoning. Let us examine this further.

As stated, an intrinsically evil act is always evil, regardless of the intention of the person performing the act or the circumstances surrounding the act. "Intrinsic" evil denotes that these acts are wrong "inside" of the act itself. This labeling of the act as intrinsically evil is different from saying it is wrong because it forbidden in the Bible or by another "extrinsic" source. The church holds then that such acts are "forbidden by God" as they "in themselves" violate the nature of persons and persons in relation to God.[19] Historically, there have been two reasons to classify an act as intrinsically evil. Such acts are wrong either by "being contrary to nature" or by "defect of right."[20] The first reason holds that there is a basic nature to humans and because of this there are basic purposes in some human actions that must be followed. For example, there are objective purposes, unitive and procreative, to the sexual act and any violation of those goes against the fundamental purpose of the act. Note the lack of biblical or theological grounding here. The second reason states that humans simply do not have the right to do these actions. That is to say, only God has the right to perform such actions, such as taking human life. If humans did this, they would be "playing God." However, one can hold that humans do not have a right to kill on nonreligious grounds as well, arguing for example on the basic goodness of human life or on grounds of ordered human relations in society.

Contemporary discussion on intrinsic evil tends to combine these two reasons. It then focuses on these actions as being antithetical to the basic purpose of morality, that is, behavior and character that essentially enhance human development or human flourishing. John Paul II, for example, writes, "Reason attests that there are objects of the human act which are by their nature 'incapable of being ordered' to God, because they radically contradict the good of the person made in his image."[21] The U.S. Catholic bishops describe intrinsic evil actions as actions that "are always incompatible with love of God and neighbor. Such actions are so deeply flawed that they are always opposed to the authentic good of persons." They directly threaten "the sanctity and dignity of human life."[22]

If intrinsic evils exist (things that by their nature are against human good and flourishing) then it would seem that there should be some things that are intrinsically good (things that by their nature promote human good and flourishing). The philosopher, William Frankena, in his classic book *Ethics*, offers the following as a possible list of intrinsic goods:

> life, consciousness, and activity; health and strength; pleasures and satisfactions of all or certain kinds; happiness, beatitude, contentment; truth; knowledge and true opinion of various kinds, understanding, wisdom; beauty, harmony, proportion in objects contemplated; aesthetic experience; morally good dispositions or virtues; mutual affection, love, friendship, cooperation; just distribution of goods and evils; harmony and proportion in one's own life; power and experiences of achievement; self-expression; freedom; peace, security; adventure and novelty; and good reputation, honor, esteem, etc.[23]

Frankena himself agrees with this list but with some qualification. He describes the goods on this list to be good "inherently" rather than "intrinsically." What is intrinsically good, he argues, is the "contemplation or experiencing" of these goods rather than the goods themselves.[24] Again, intrinsic refers to the thing being good "on the inside of itself." This is a permanent feature of the thing. Inherent refers to persons participating in some way with these goods.

Frankena's reflection on intrinsic good and the relationship to personal experience is very important. First, this reminds us that morality is more than "do not do bad things." Human flourishing is ultimately about reaching for the heights of existence and meaning in life, not merely the simple foundations of life. Additionally, Frankena's list reminds us that these goods are good "for us" as individuals and groups. We can say that the opposite is true as we consider intrinsic evils. The fundamental point of calling something an intrinsic evil is that it harms both the person performing the act, as well as the victim of the act. Indeed by performing the act and harming oneself, the person may also be the "victim" of the act. Recall that long list of evils quoted above from John Paul II. The paragraph in the original text concludes, "They contaminate those who inflict them more than those who suffer injustice."[25] Performing an intrinsic evil harms the personality of the person performing the act.

The concept that some acts are intrinsically evil is a controversial one. My guess is that while all people would think that some acts are intrinsically evil (who, for example, could justify rape or genocide?), not everyone would agree that all the acts listed above are intrinsically evil (mutilation and deportation seem vague descriptions of moral actions). That is to say, some people would hold that some intentions and within some circumstances, a particular action listed above might not be always wrong to perform. Thus the actions are not wrong "in themselves."

The term intrinsic evil is longstanding in moral theology. Some of the acts it references are clearly acts performed by individuals. They are personal acts. Many of these acts, however, are more complicated. Groups, such as nations and corporations, perform them. In the minds of many people, these acts are understandable but unfortunate consequences of real life. Some may note that slavery or discrimination against women is cultural or part of social practice. Some may describe war or torture or arbitrary imprisonment as political realities that we have to live with. Some may not be as concerned by subhuman living conditions nor disgraceful working conditions, as they are said to be byproducts of economic realities. By this thinking, we will always have abortion and we will always have prostitution. Thus we see the contemporary use of the phrase intrinsic evil. In the past, the phrase has been part of moral theology's ethical reflection. Today, it has become part of the tradition's prophetic discourse. It has been used to stir the conscience of people. "NO!" it says, these things are wrong!

When we reflect on personal acts, such as yelling at your roommate or stealing from her, we can clearly address the questions of responsibility and accountability. It is not so clear in the case of many of the intrinsic evils. I can say that I do not discriminate and that I have never created subhuman living conditions nor I have never tortured anybody. Yet I do fully participate in our economy of consumerism. I eat food, wear clothes, own and use electronics produced around the world within all sorts of working conditions that I would never work in. My lifestyle contributes to the suffering of others. William Cavanaugh's pithy description of this worldview, which is detached, on a global scale, from the production and indeed the producers of all our daily goods, is, "We shop; they drop."[26]

I think Cathleen Kaveny is correct in her thinking here. She argues that as prophetic language, the public discussion of intrinsic evils is "evocative, not analytical."[27] Prophetic language is crucial to moral theology as it pushes "people of goodwill" into needed discussions about "grave injustices of the world."[28] It stops and makes me think, for example, about my consumer habits. But like Amos' "let justice roll down like waters," the language of intrinsic evil "does not help us with the practical analysis" needed to make policy. It "does not advance our judgment about whether the most effect way to combat that practice is by the enactment of legal strictures."[29] It does, however, grab our attention and push us into ethical discourse and then, at some level, to policy discourse. But it is not policy discourse.

We can say six things about the concept of intrinsically evil acts. The first is that they bring real harm to the person acting and the person receiving the action (even an act of self-mutilation or suicide harms others). The second is that these acts are always wrong.

The third is that not all intrinsically evil acts are morally equivalent.[30] There are "greater" and "lesser" evils. Smoking a cigarette is not the same as bombing a city. The fourth is that the categorization of something as an intrinsic evil is controversial. The categorization assumes the full range of intentions within circumstances. That is to say, if one could think of a time and intention in which the act described as an intrinsic evil is actually morally neutral or indeed a morally good thing, then it is not an intrinsic evil. It may, however, be an act that is usually always wrong or nearly absolutely wrong. The fifth point here is that the human-centered description of evil is not adequate. This description has to be expanded to include some acts that bring harm to nonhuman elements of creation. Most people would agree, for example, that torturing animals is intrinsically wrong. Many would add that human acts that compromise the particular environment that a species is dependent on for survival also would count as intrinsically evil. Finally, the language of intrinsic evil can be prophetic as well as ethical, stirring the consciences of people to confront evil, evil often embedded in "normal" cultural practices.

Clearly Defining an Action

Most everyone would strongly hold "Do not kill" as a moral rule, yet many of those same people (except my pacifist friends) would say that that rule admits to many exceptions. Think of the possibilities of so-called "justifiable" killing. Do you think in some instances it is morally legitimate to kill another in self-defense? Do you think that some wars are morally appropriate? Do you think that in some cases capital punishment is morally legitimate? If you answer "Yes" to any of these questions, then you do not hold the rule "Do not kill" to be absolute. Yet, you probably recognize the vital importance of this rule in everyday life. This rule is more than just a guideline or a suggestion. You might say that the rule is "nearly" absolute.

In the legal tradition, there is a phrase used to describe rules like "Do not kill." These rules are said to be *prima facie* absolute. *Prima facie* is a Latin phrase that means literally "at first face" or better stated, "at first glance." "Do not kill" is a moral rule that, at first glance, seems absolute. Yet when one looks more closely at the rule, one could foresee some very limited situations in which the rule can be justifiably overridden. If the rule is to be overridden, it is up to those who want to override it to prove that the exception is morally justified. What would such a "proof" look like? Traditionally it has been called the "principle of double effect."

People generally credit St. Thomas Aquinas with the initial description of the "principle of double effect" (although he himself never refers to this as such).[31] As he examines the question of self-defense, St. Thomas challenges the view of his great predecessor, St. Augustine. In a famous discussion in *On Free Choice of the Will*, Augustine argues that it is wrong to kill another in self-defense (although he is not against all killing, nor is he against all wars).[32] St. Thomas addresses this question with the interesting proposition: "I answer that there is nothing to prevent one act from having two effects, of which only one is intended by the agent and the other is outside of his intention." He continues, "Now, moral actions receive their character according to what is intended." When a person acts to defend oneself, "A twofold effect can follow: one, the saving of one's own life; the other, the killing of the aggressor." This act can be moral; however, not all acts of killing in self-defense are moral. St. Thomas notes that the act itself must be "proportioned to the end intended."[33] Thus, "if one uses greater violence than is necessary in defending his own life," the act would be immoral.[34]

In the centuries following Aquinas moral theologians advanced and clarified his argument. Joseph Mangan, in a 1949 article, presented the definitive description of the principle: "A person may licitly perform an action that he foresees will produce a good effect and a bad effect provided that four conditions are verified at one and the same time: (1) that the action in itself from its very object be good or at least indifferent; (2) that the good effect and not the evil effect be intended; (3) that the good effect be not produced by means of the evil effect; (4) that there be a proportionately grave reason for permitting the evil effect."[35]

Note the priority of intention in understanding the morality of the act. As Thomas says, "moral actions receive their character according to what is intended." Note also the role of proportionate reason. Finally, according to Mangan, the four stated criteria are mutually informative rather than separate rules. Thus the principle ought to be understood as a "guide to prudent moral judgment" rather than an "inflexible rule or mathematical formula."[36]

The first condition sets the limits of the principle and helps to define the nature of an act. I want to present some very simple situations to illustrate this. Let's say you are being attacked. You act to stop the attack. Your action, hitting or harming the other, must first and foremost be understood as an act that defends, not as an act that attacks. You are protecting yourself and at the same time hurting the attacker. That is to say, if you were not directly attacked at that moment and you acted to harm another person, you could not justify the act. The act would then be an act not of defense but of aggression. Think of this in another way: if a person harmed or threatened to harm you yesterday and you met him today and then harmed him, your act is not an act of self-defense. It would be better classified as an act of revenge.

The second condition concerns intention. An example often given to discuss the principle is the case of the soldier who throws himself on a landmine so as to save the lives of his platoon members. One might say that he kills himself, but that is not a true description of the act. As with the act of self-defense, the intention makes the act. The act was an act to protect the lives and well-being of the members of the platoon.

The third condition looks at the evil effect. This is a hard condition to understand. Remember that, as Mangan suggests, one must consider all four together for one judgment. This is not a checklist. The third condition states that one cannot do evil for a good effect. Thus the principle of the double effect is not a form of simple consequentialist reasoning. For the consequentialist, only the consequences of the act matter for moral reflection. We have already noted here, however, that it is the intention that gives the moral character to the act. When one "does" something, one performs an action and an intention. The "good" action includes a good intention. The "evil" action includes the evil intention (unless, of course, the act is intrinsically evil). As Mangan writes, "if the cause directly produces the evil effect and produces the good effect only by means of the evil effect, then the good is sought by willing the evil."[37] Note that importance of cause and effect here. There was one act and two effects. Consider the "double effect" of an act of self-defense. When you hit another person (the act) you, at the same time protect your life (first effect) and you bring physical harm to the other (second effect).

The final condition is proportionality. Your response to the aggressor must be proportionate to the aggression. If the aggressor is merely verbally aggressive, killing in self-defense is disproportionate. Consider another example. At times it is justifiable for police officers to use lethal force. At other times it is not. Some of this depends on the nature of the aggression or the threat of the aggression. Violent acts by police officers that are disproportionate to the aggression are justifiably considered "police brutality."

The principle of the double effect highlights the link between the elements of the three-font principle. The meaning of many "acts" cannot be understood by the physical act alone. If I gave you a picture of someone punching another person, your *prima facie* response would be that it is wrong. But you really would not know the true nature of the act without knowing the intention and the circumstances. The act might be an act of aggression (wrong) or an act of revenge (wrong) or it may be an act of self-defense (it may be wrong or it may not—see Mangan's four elements for objective criteria for such a judgment).

All of this is to say that as one reflects on morality, we are confronted by the reality that the human purposeful action is complex.

Consider lying. In her classic book on the subject, *Lying*, Sissela Bok defines a lie as "an intentionally deceptive message in the form of a statement."[38] Everybody "knows" lying is wrong. There are prohibitions against lying, for example, in the Ten Commandments and in just about anyone's set of moral rules.[39] Lying manipulates and limits the freedom of another. When you lie you aim to control another's relationship to the truth and thus his or her ability to choose. This intention and goal are harmful to them. When you lie, moreover, you distort the sense of truth and justice within yourself. As you lie, you become a certain "sort-of-person" generally know as a "liar."

Lying is against the entire range of moral expectations (rules, intentions/goals, and virtue). It also is an unjust interference in the freedom of others. Yet there are social and pragmatic reasons against lying as well. Would you want to live in a world where family, friends, teachers, employers, salespersons, employees, police officers, bus drivers, doctors, ministers, might tell you the truth some of the time? A world like that would be very hard to live and flourish in. Lying, then, is wrong. The severity of the wrong (remember smoking versus bombing a civilian center) depends, however, on the intention of the person lying and indeed the circumstances of the lie. Yet the problem of the "justifiable" lie lingers. You perhaps have lied to another and not thought it was wrong. On the other hand, have you ever been lied to? Did you feel that the lie was justified?

In *Lying,* Bok considers the range of possible circumstances and intentions that some people might think would allow for exceptions to the rule against lying. Her list includes "white" lies, lies in times of crisis, lies to liars, lies to enemies, lies to protect others, lies for the public good, paternalistic lies, and lies to the sick and dying.[40] A strong argument can be made that in all of these situations, lying is wrong. But it is interesting to note that in all of these acts multiple intentions and indeed multiple "effects" are present.

Think about what we call "white" lies. When you tell a white lie you intend to deceive a person but at the same time you intend to be nice to the person. This sense of multiple intentions is at the heart of the issue and indeed the heart of judging moral actions. For example, your friend asks you if she looks good in her new dress. You think the dress is ugly but you tell her you think she looks good. You are a liar but your friend feels better. The wrong of this lie is minimal. Yet her freedom is in a sense diminished as she lacks important information in her decision about what to wear.

What does this mean for you? Earlier in the book we talked about character traits, and how our actions flow from our internal dispositions and traits. That is to say, our actions come from the sorts of persons we are. The opposite of this is also true. Our actions, particularly ones repeated over time, form our internal dispositions.

Cathleen Kaveny comments, "Deliberately performing an evil act warps an agent's character, distorting his capacity to . . . follow through on good choices in the future."[41] She compares "moral fitness" to physical fitness. "Eating only junk food and shunning exercise leads to a loss of the taste for more nutritious food."[42] The "couch potato" is unlikely to want to go on a long walk in the woods. "Similarly," she argues, "regularly performing" evil acts "can make one less able to recognize morally virtuous acts, and less able to perform them when they are required."[43]

Let's return to white lies. If you lied to your friend once, is it easier to lie to her about something else in the future? If you lie to your friend about a simple thing like a dress in order to help her feel good, what will you do about more complex things? Let's flip the questions around. If she found out you lied to her, can she trust you in the future? In a small way, you harmed yourself (internally and in your relation to her) for convenience over truth.

Sin

If this book were simply about morality, we could move on to the next chapter, but it is not. It is about Christian morality. Harmful acts (in the full sense of the term to include intentions), that is to say, acts that harm the dignity of persons (including yourself) are more than they seem. They not only disrupt the proper order of your relationships to yourself, and your relationships to others, they also harm your relationship to God. Such harmful acts, to use the appropriate theological word, are sins.

The idea of sin is hard to define and perhaps hard to fit into the modern context. We live in sort of a "sin-free world" empowered by three vague ideas. The first is the modern myth that human moral progress mirrors human technological progress. We tend to think of our generation as "more moral" than the previous generations. Sin loses its bite. We, after all, do not have slaves and women can vote! The second vague idea is a view that because God's love is (so-called) unconditional, God expects nothing of us. God loves us, so it's all good. This contemporary view transforms Augustine's famous line, "Love and do what you will" into "God loves you so do what you will."

Here again, sin loses its bite. A third idea is the contemporary turn from rule-based morality to virtue-based morality. The generalization today is that "back in the day" morality was all about rules, but modern morality is all about being "good people." If what matters is our general confidence and sense of striving to be good and being directed to God, sin again loses its bite. All this is to say that sin often seems more like a medieval word than a living word.

Added to the modern loss of a sense of sin is the problematic idea of sin itself. For such a historically strong idea, it is rather hard to define. As Darlene Fozard Weaver writes in her discussion of sin and the moral life, "Attempts to identify one foundational or overarching figure for sin are unnecessary and ill advised."[44] In one paragraph, for example, the *Catechism* describes sin as an "offense against God," a turning away from "God's love," "disobedience" against God, a "revolt against God," "contempt of God," "proud self-exaltation," and "diametrically opposed to the obedience of Jesus."[45] Note that these definitions all address the internal disposition of the person that is expressed in the external action.

There are other ways to define sin. In his book *Sin: A History*, Gary Anderson argues that biblical texts use metaphors to capture the essence of sin: "Sins are like stains that require cleansing, burdens that must be removed, or debts that have to be repaid."[46] The biblical images Anderson cites highlight what happens as a result of sin. As Anderson writes, "Human sins have consequences. When individuals disobey moral law, a tangible form of evil is created in the world that must be accounted for."[47] Anderson points to a bold example of the consequences of sin. He writes, "And this is even more true when a whole society goes astray. One recalls the horrible sin of slavery in this country in the seventeenth and eighteenth centuries. It is a demonstrable fact the American culture has paid deeply for this travesty and continues to do so."[48]

Weaver also highlights the consequences of sin. As she describes the various kinds of sins, for example infidelity and falsehood, she notes the "disorienting, debilitating, and disintegrating effects" of sin.[49] She writes, "Sin mars the world" and "weakens our moral reflection."[50]

The Pontifical Biblical Commission likewise describes the consequences of sin in its study of morality and the Bible. The Commission writes, "Evil deeds produce cosmic distortion. They go against the order of creation, and balance can be regained only through actions that restore the world order."[51] This view of sin is key to understanding God's mercy. God, the Commission argues, is a "benevolent Creator who restores human beings to their pristine condition of being loved by him, and mends the damage inflicted on the cosmos."[52]

Anderson's discussion of the consequences of the sin of slavery reminds us that sin cannot simply be described in direct-relational terms: You steal money from your roommate. People can sin by supporting the sinful activities of others. They can sin by refraining from acting in the face of evil. Their fear or indifference or silence or apathy can be sinful. This category of indirect and perhaps impersonal sin is called "social sin."[53] It is often characterized, in the words of Martin Luther King Jr., by the "silence of good people"[54] "more devoted to 'order' than to justice."[55] Persons create patterns of social action that tend to justify harm and evil or displace accountability and responsibility—thus the need for prophetic moral discourse.

The strength of using a metaphor to describe a complex reality is that it can communicate a truth about the reality if the reader has some knowledge or experience of the reference. In this spirit I would make a comment on the *Catechism's* words. My comments do not reject the truth of their statements, but question the communicative adequacy of such descriptions. When I reflect on my sinfulness and the many times I have sinned, I do not see myself revolting against God. I do not have contempt for God, nor am I purposefully turning away from God's love.

I do, however, feel as if I harmed my relationship with God, much like if I hurt a loved one or a friend or a colleague. In acting inappropriately, I do not have contempt for them and I am not revolting against them. I am stupidly and selfishly acting without regard for them as persons and without regard for the good that is our relationship. I think there is then something to be said about the notions of sin that highlight the consequences of sin. When we harm our relationships we feel the burden or the stain on our hearts. Harming your relationship with God is the essence of sin.

I find Thomas Aquinas's discussion on love and friendship with God helpful here. Aquinas offers *caritas*, a particular form of love, as a description of the fundamental relationship between people and God. *Caritas*, Thomas says, is friendship with God. In this relationship, God's love for us is stable, strong, and passionate. We cannot, however, say the same about our love for God. We are fickle, weak, and drawn to relationships to other things and persons that distract us from what we ought to love. Thomas says that through a single act, a mortal sin, we can break our relationship to God. It is much more often the case, however, that we slowly push ourselves away from God. He writes, "For God does not turn away from man, more than man turns away from Him."[56] But then we can always make the choice to turn back.

When I do something that harms another, such as I lie to him or her, I must respond to restore the break. The first step is to honestly reflect on my action and acknowledge to myself that it was wrong. Weaver describes this as "naming the action."[57] Seeking forgiveness and accepting forgiveness can then follow. But the action is not simply interior; harm may call for restorative actions (good intentions, good actions, within appropriate circumstances) that acknowledge the harm.

True restorative actions in relationships have at least two purposes. First, they are expressions of the fundamental gratitude I have for the other's love for and commitment to me even when I have failed. Second, such actions make me vulnerable so as to help me accept their love, love that in some ways I do not deserve. (I might add, however, that a dozen red roses *complementing* my gratitude and openness never hurts!)

There is something similar to repairing a damaged relationship and my sin. That is to say, to repairing my damaged *caritas*. I cannot "do" anything to win God's love. At the same time, I am compelled to act as I recognize the reality of the situation. God's forgiveness already exists. Weaver describes this well: "God already loves us *in* our sinfulness. There is nothing about us that requires or deserves forgiveness, and yet God not only endowed us with intrinsic worth, God longs to enter into the mess we are and have made so as to draw us out of it. God compassionately responds to our sinfulness and delights in showing us mercy."[58] I appreciate her words here. People who acknowledge their sins often feel that they have created a "mess."

Recognition of my sin and God's forgiveness compel me to act to restore the relationship that has disintegrated. True restorative acts then serve two purposes. First, *they help me* to be more able to see God's love in the world and to receive God's love. In Aquinas's words, such acts "dispose" me "to receive the infusion of" *caritas*.[59] God may love me but I have to open the door to let that love in. Second, contrary to what some might think, these acts are not intended to buy God off or to "influence his will to pardon" me.[60] These restorative acts are *expressions that I accept* God's forgiveness. A dozen prayers or a dozen good works without such intentions "do" nothing.

Actions matter and sin is real. After affirming this we can recognize that persons matter more over actions and forgiveness is the final word over sin. We make many singular acts every day that form our life narrative. The particular choice in each action is yours and thus the particular choice in the form of your life narrative is yours. Choose well.

Thinking of the Whole, Not Only the Parts

This chapter has been an invitation to reflect on the morality of human action. It is fundamentally a reflection on the power we have in our choices. While actions have consequences, they also have sources. Reflection on human action always returns to the source, the internal power we all have to direct our being and our doing in one way or another. Reflection on human action invites the deeper question of moral identity. This chapter has suggested that the three-font principle is helpful in this refection with the caveat that actions ultimately find their meaning in the life narrative of the person (the four-font principle). Moral theology is not simply about particular acts, although all persons ought to reflect on their behavior. Moral theology is fundamentally about the narrative of persons' lives and how particular acts fit within those narratives. Moral theology is about the totality of persons' lives and relationships.

We addressed the question of intrinsically evil acts (and the related question of absolute moral rules) and the complex problem that human action often results from a variety of intentions. The question of intrinsic evil is important, both philosophically and personally. Are there acts that you would never perform, that are, in essence, intrinsically evil for you? There have to be some. I am not thinking about public policy or legislating morality here. I am thinking of concrete acts that you would never do. If your friends or loved ones did them, you would be very disappointed. Persons with any sense of moral identity know that there are certain things they would never do. On the flip side of this, which of Frankena's intrinsic goods would you say are most important to you at this time in your life? Which of these are crucial to your flourishing as a person? There must be some. Which might you wish to develop in the future?

We ended with a short discussion on sin and the possibility of restorative acts. The truest thing we can say about immoral acts is that they harm the person doing them and through them the person pushes away from God. The truest thing we can say about sinning is that it does not have to be the final word.

Questions

1. Explain the three-font principle and discuss its strengths and weaknesses.

2. Explain the notion of an intrinsically evil act in relation to the three-font principle. Give either an example of an intrinsically evil act and explain why you would classify it as such or explain why you think the category of intrinsic evil is not helpful.

3. A lie is an "intentionally deceptive message in the form of a state-ment." Can lies be justified by the three-font principle or are all lies intrinsically evil? Explain your thinking.

4. Does the notion of *prima facie* evil help thinking in moral theol-ogy? Give a reason for your evaluation.

5. Think of a sin as an act of distorted love. Explain then how sin (negatively) relates to the characteristics of love described in the previous chapter.

6. This book is about moral theology and, not surprisingly, the author uses biblical and other religious sources to develop ideas. The author also uses nonreligious sources to develop ideas. Dis-cuss how and why the author uses nonreligious sources in this chapter.

CHAPTER FIVE

Conscience

And went on thinking. And got to thinking over our trip down the river; and I see Jim before me all the time: in the day and in the nighttime, sometimes moonlight, sometimes storms, and we a-floating along, talking and singing and laughing. But somehow I couldn't seem to strike no places to harden me against him, but only the other kind. I'd see him standing my watch on top of his'n, stead of calling me, so I could go on sleeping; and see him how glad he was when I come back out of the fog . . . and [he] said I was the best friend old Jim ever had in the world, and the only one he's got now; and then I happened to look around and see that paper. It was a close place. I took it up, and held it in my hand. I was a-trembling, because I'd got to decide, forever, betwixt two things, and I knowed it. I studied a minute, sort of holding my breath, and then says to myself: "All right, then, I'll go to hell"—and tore it up.

—Huck Finn in Mark Twain, *Adventures of Huckleberry Finn* [1]

Examine yourselves . . . Test yourselves.
—St. Paul, 2 Corinthians, 13:5

This is my prayer, that your love may overflow more and more with knowledge and full insight to help you determine what is best.
—St. Paul, Philippians 1:9–10

In an earlier chapter we read the story of the Good Samaritan and noted that the priest and the Levite choose the "lesser part." It did not have to be that way. The priest could have helped the wounded man, and the Samaritan could have ignored him. That, of course, would have given us a different story ("The Parable of the Good Priest and Bad Samaritan"). The point here is that the priest, Levite, and Samaritan all made choices. They could have acted differently, but somewhere in their "hearts" they decided to act as they did. Simply

141

put, they all had the freedom to act and they all acted out of their freedoms. The objective of this chapter is to describe what is meant by the idea that "somewhere in their hearts they decided to act." Our topic is conscience and the aim of the chapter is to explore the ways people experience having a conscience. This is not an easy task. As Richard Gula remarks, "Trying to explain conscience is like trying to nail jello to the wall; just when you think you have pinned it down, part of it begins to slip away."[2]

The three quotations beginning this chapter all deal with conscience. The first is a classic scene in Mark Twain's *Adventures of Huckleberry Finn.* Here is the context: It is Missouri in the 1830s and the boy Huck Finn is traveling with Jim, a runaway slave. By the social and religious standards of his day, Huck is required to turn Jim in. Twain, however, depicts Huck as a boy with unusually strong moral identity, as a person with a developed conscience. Huck sees Jim not as a piece of property to be owned by another but as a person, indeed as a friend. His conscience demands that he reject the social norms. He decides not to turn Jim in, and instead to suffer the consequences. The second two quotations are from St. Paul in the New Testament. They highlight important features of conscience, namely, self-reflection, the need to gather knowledge, and the importance of gaining insight. Most importantly Paul suggests his listeners develop overflowing love.

In this chapter we will pick up the themes from the opening quotations, beginning with a discussion of popular mistaken views of conscience. Then we can consider the question of whether or not everyone has a conscience. This chapter suggests that we experience conscience in four ways. The final section moves from the personal to the social and argues that our communities often need persons who act like a conscience for the whole.

Mistaken Views of Conscience

Many people confuse the word "conscience" with the word conscious. The words are related but distinct. *Conscious* refers to the state of being aware and alert. You have to be conscious to read this sentence. When a person loses consciousness or becomes unconscious, she is not responsive to stimuli and is not aware of herself or her environment. For conscience to function, in fact, the person must be conscious. Note what the word conscience literally means. "Con" means with and "science" means knowledge; conscience means then "with knowledge." Being "with knowledge," using one's conscience, implies being aware of oneself, conscious, and having a level of functioning mental processes.[3] The more one's conscience is developed, the deeper one's consciousness, one's awareness of oneself, others, and the environments in which we live. The fundamental "knowledge" of conscience, then, is oneself and the context in which one finds oneself.

There are deeper misunderstandings of conscience than simply confusing it with being conscious. There are at least three "reductionistic" views of conscience in contemporary conversations. These views of conscience are reductionistic because, while they have some truth to them, they reduce the full meaning of conscience to one part. Perhaps the most common reductionistic view states that conscience is "nothing but" *subjective* or *individualist feelings* about one's actions. In this view, conscience is simply my standards for morality based on my experience. Again, there is a part of this view that is correct, conscience is certainly a subjective experience that includes feelings. Yet it is fundamentally more than that.

Conscience is a place of inquiry, knowledge, and understanding. It is a decision-making place and not simply a "follow your feelings" place. It is personal but ultimately it is not individualistic. In the words of moral theologian Darlene Fozard Weaver, "Conscience does not create right and wrong, but witnesses to an objective moral law that confronts and obliges the person."[4] That is to say, my conscience stands in relation to a moral order outside myself. It is my response to the objective good.

Gula neatly summarizes the nonindividualistic yet highly personal characteristic of conscience when he notes, "A criterion of mature moral conscience is the ability to make up one's mind for oneself about what ought to be done. Note: The criterion say *for* oneself, not *by* oneself."[5]

If there are people who hold that conscience is wholly individualistic, there are also some people who deny the individualism of conscience. A second type of reductionism is psychological or sociological reductionism. This says that conscience is "nothing but" the *superego*. The superego is the ego of "another superimposed on our own to serve as an internal censor to regulate our conduct."[6] There is no doubt that individuals, society, culture, communities, and authorities do influence our conscience. But to say that the voice of society is my conscience belittles the experience of the thinking, reflecting self. As Joseph Ratzinger wrote: "First, conscience is not identical to personal wishes and taste. Secondly, conscience cannot be reduced to social advantage, to group consensus or to the demands of political and social power."[7] While one's conscience has intimate connections to external authorities, the mature conscience ultimately is personal. In the words of Gula, "For moral maturity one must be one's own person. . . . The morally mature adult is called to commit his or her freedom, not to submit it."[8]

Another reductionistic view of conscience comes from the study of evolutionary psychology. This view holds that what we call conscience is "nothing but" the *instincts that have evolved within humans.* These instincts have allowed us to develop and maintain social relations and to ensure the preservation of the species. Morality, according to some commentators, appears "to have deep evolutionary roots."[9] Yet there is more to morality and to conscience than what can be explained by our inherited moral sense.[10] Conscience is creative and, indeed, following one's conscience might not always lead to self-protection and comfort.

Reductionistic views of conscience reject freedom. If conscience is "nothing but" our feelings or a moral authority's voice within us or the result of human evolution, then we really do not have freedom to choose and work toward complex goods, nor do we have the freedom to choose the sorts of persons we want to become. You can and do choose complex goods for yourself and you have a certain control over the sort of person you want to be.

Does Everyone Have a Conscience?

Most people would agree with two statements about conscience. The first is that when they meet a person, they assume that person has a conscience. Secondly, they believe that one's conscience is not necessarily a finished product. I have heard people compare a conscience to a garden. Like a garden, a conscience needs to be tended if it is to become what it is meant to be. Theologian John Mahoney is quite right when he says that we should be responsible *to* our conscience and that we also must be responsible *for* our conscience. The morally mature person takes responsibility for the development of one's conscience. Mahoney notes that what one puts into one's conscience, one gets out of one's conscience. As he says, "garbage in, garbage out."[11] On the other hand, love in, love out!

But does everyone have a conscience? Newborn babies and young children do not have a conscience in the normal sense of the word. Perhaps we can say that they have the potential for a conscience. They cannot reflect on their actions. They are not "free" to choose simple or complex goods or the sorts of persons they want to be. Thus we do not hold them responsible for their actions until they have reached a minimal moral maturity. I will defer questions about what age this happens to others (there are reasons why we have age restrictions on marriage, driving, voting, drinking, and serving in the military, and why we have juvenile courts, as well as why auto insurance rates go down at age twenty-five).

It is thought that psychopaths do not have a conscience. Robert Hare, for example, opens his book *Without Conscience* with the following: "Psychopaths are social predators who charm, manipulate, and ruthlessly plow their way through life, leaving a broad trail of broken hearts, shattered expectations, and empty wallets. Completely lacking in conscience and in feelings for others, they selfishly take what they want and do as they please, violating social norms and expectations without the slightest sense of guilt or regret."[12]

Psychopaths choose their actions, but they knowingly violate rules and persons *without feelings for others or feeling guilt or regret*. This is a key point. There may be a variety of causes for this. An accident may have caused brain damage and impaired functioning of a person. Children left to die or placed in situations where they were unable to bond with others may be developmentally impaired as adults. If persons never develop relationships of care and trust with others, how can they feel bad when they hurt others? That is to say, how can they develop a mature conscience?

Elie Wiesel, the survivor and truth-teller of the Holocaust, considers a tougher question. What about "good" people who seem to act without a conscience in particular parts of their lives? He wonders how and why Nazi doctors turned into killers. Wiesel writes, "Instead of doing their job, instead of bringing assistance and comfort to the sick people who needed them most, instead of helping the mutilated and the handicapped to live, eat, and hope one more day, one more hour, doctors became their executioners."[13] He continues, "After Germany's defeat, with rare exceptions, criminal doctors calmly returned home to resume normal practices and ordinary life."[14] Wiesel shockingly notes that the Nazi doctors held a distinct position in the camps. They were not soldiers subject to commanders. They could have acted differently. Why did they torture and kill during the war and live like "normal" doctors after the war? Wiesel writes that the doctors saw themselves as patriots and scientists.[15] He also wonders how American doctors could have overseen the torture of prisoners in Guantanamo Bay detention camp.

I cannot fully understand, but I can accept, the idea that some people do not "have" a conscience. I have a very hard time, however, accepting the fact that people who "have" a conscience in most parts of their lives seem not to have a conscience in particular parts of their lives. Stepping back from these two scenarios, one can see some sort of a link. In both situations there is a shocking lack of *feelings for others* or *feeling guilt or regret*.

Some commentators speak of levels or types of feelings for others. The most basic, they say, is sympathy. Sympathy is "a feeling of sorrow for the plight of another . . . pity at another's need."[16] The development of one's conscience depends on one's ability to have sympathy. "With knowledge" then means with knowledge of the suffering of another person. The maturing conscience grows from sympathy to deeper levels of feeling. Sympathy can develop into empathy. When one has empathy, one identifies with the needs of the other. Compassion takes the person to yet a deeper level of engagement with the other. When one has compassion, one experiences both sorrow and identification, plus one feels the need to respond to the other. "Compassion acts to alleviate the suffering of another."[17] The Good Samaritan had compassion and Jesus tells his listeners to "Go and do likewise."

For me, a striking summary of this compassion is found in the opening line of *Gaudium et Spes*: "The joys and the hopes, the griefs and the anxieties of the men [and women] of this age, especially those who are poor or in any way afflicted, these are the joys and hopes, the griefs and anxieties of the followers of Christ."[18]

The move from sympathy to empathy to compassion is accompanied by the deepening of one's consciousness, that is to say, one's awareness of oneself and others. With this awareness comes a growing sense of relationality and responsibility toward others. Mark Twain's description of Huck Finn's decision is a moving illustration of a person captured by compassion. Compassion makes him conscious of the moral demands placed on him as he sees Jim as a person.

To push the garden metaphor of conscience (perhaps a bit too much), the seedling is sympathy, the growing plant is empathy, and the flower is compassion. We are responsible for the growth of this plant. But as Martha Nussbaum reminded us in chapter 2, this is not simply something one does alone. We need to be informed and formed by others. In order for me to be compassionate, I need to see compassion modeled in the lives of others. In order for me to be compassionate, I need to be supported by others. I do it with and among others. I come to know compassion when people show it to me.

If we do not or cannot see others and ourselves as persons (in the fullest sense of the term), there can be no sympathy and there will never be empathy or compassion. The most fundamental knowledge of conscience is the personal acknowledgement that all humans are persons and their personhood makes demands on us. The primary demand is that we see that the other is more like us than different from us. Persons who "have" a conscience in parts of their lives but not in the whole of their lives assign the status of personhood to a limited number of humans of their choosing. This is rightly called "prejudice" that leads to racism and sexism.

Christian morality is demanding. Sympathy, empathy, and compassion are not enough! Beyond compassion lies solidarity, the "effort to build a human community where every social group participates equitably in social life and contributes its genius for the good of all."[19] In the words of John Paul II, solidarity "is a firm and persevering determination to commit oneself to the common good . . . because we are all really responsible for all. . . . [It is] a commitment to the good of one's neighbor with the readiness, in the gospel sense, to 'lose oneself' for the sake of the other."[20] Solidarity pushes us to see others not as objects or impersonal beings or faceless humans, but as our neighbors. Solidarity causes a "religious awareness" in persons. "One's neighbor is then not only a human being with his or her own rights and a fundamental equality with everyone else, but becomes the living image of God the Father. . . . One's neighbor must therefore be loved, even if an enemy, with the same love with which the Lord loves him or her."[21]

If conscience means "with knowledge," one might expand that to mean "with knowledge of the heart." Fundamentally, there are four parts of this knowledge. The first is the knowledge of the experiences of one's self and one's context. The second is the knowledge of the experience of one's internal freedoms (for simple goods, complex goods, and for the sort of person one wants to be). The third knowledge is the experience of others as persons (moving from sympathy to compassion). The fourth type of knowledge is the experience that the first three compel one to be a certain sort of person who does certain sorts of actions. Note the convergence of the "subjective" and the "objective" in these four parts. Each refers to a personal experience of something "beyond" oneself. Those who are said to have "no" conscience (because of deliberate life choices or unfortunate situations) seem to be lacking in each of these areas.

The Four Features of Conscience

Many movies and books have conscience as their central theme. The main character must make a decision, not an ordinary decision, but a decision that has significant consequences. While the decision seems at first to be about something the character should do or not do, in reality, the decision is ultimately about who the character is as a person. That is the point. At the end of the day, the conscience is more about who you are as a person than the particular choices you make. This being said, we will look at the ways people experience having a conscience.

Have you felt bad or guilty when you have done something wrong or when you hurt another person? Have you ever felt good after doing something nice for another person? If you have, you have a conscience. These experiences point to a very popular way of understanding conscience. Your conscience is that faculty inside of you that sparks feelings, positive and negative, in response to your actions. A second question: Have you ever had to make a decision where you needed to take some time to think things through? You may have needed some space to work through your feelings, goals, and possible choices. If you have, you have a conscience. Your conscience is that process where you reflect on your choices, where you discern appropriate action. A third question: Have you ever just sat quietly, thinking or dreaming or praying, wondering about who you are and where you will be in a few years? If you have, you have a conscience. Conscience can be thought of as that internal "place" where you go when you seek some solitude or peace. Conscience is where you pray, where you talk to God. Finally, have you ever simply felt, without much thinking, that you had to do something or that you should not do something? Have you ever felt an impulse to do the right thing that seemed natural or spontaneous to you? If you have, you have a conscience. Conscience is that faculty inside us that compels us to act or not to act. Some people describe this to be a "voice" inside them directing their action.

People experience their conscience in at least four ways.[22] To limit the idea of the conscience to being only one of these four elements, however, misses the full sense of what the conscience is. Some might think of it only as a source of guilt when you do something wrong. But feelings of guilt or, on the other hand, the feeling of peace, are results of something other than themselves. Put simply, they "come" from somewhere. Thus the idea that conscience is a "place." One might say that this is the antecedent[23] conscience, as it in a sense precedes the thinking and the feeling. Others tend to think of conscience only as the decision-making part of us. Yet we do feel things as a result of our decisions and we also experience some sort of center or core of our being where we make our decisions. Television and film have certainly popularized the notion that conscience is a voice inside of us. Yet again, if we do experience a moral impulse or voice, we know that it is produced by something. Again, a full understanding of conscience includes all four of the elements. Thus, we will use the word "conscience" broadly here. We will hold it to describe these four fundamental "moral" experiences we all have.

Conscience then refers to the *source of feelings* that spring up in us as a consequence of our actions. It also refers to the reflective *process* of working through a decision. Conscience is that "*place*" within us; and it refers to the strong sense, or *voice*, we have at times directing us to do or not do something. Conscience, then, is a crucial, perhaps the crucial, element of the moral life. Indeed we could not speak about the moral life without including conscience.

Conscience as a Source of Feelings

Our strongest experiences of conscience have to do with feelings. "Feelings" is to be understood in two ways here. The first has to do with feeling the feelings of others. Indeed as we noted earlier, people who lack a conscience or lack a strong conscience are said to be without feelings for others. They do not have guilt or regret when they harm others. Thus we described the moral movement from sympathy to compassion and solidarity. Recall the quote from *Gaudium et Spes*: The joys, hopes, griefs, and anxieties of people, particularly the afflicted, *are the* joys, hopes, griefs, and anxieties of Christians. This first sense of feelings stands as a rejection of individualistic notions of conscience. When you "feel" the joys and sufferings of another you are confronted by objective reality of the other.

Yet there is another equally important role for feelings in the conscience. Conscience is the source of the feelings that arise in a person on account of his or her choices. This aspect of conscience can be called "consequent" conscience. Such feelings are the result of some action or choice. Simply stated, conscience is the source of happiness and joy when you do the right thing and make good decisions. Likewise it is the source of remorse or guilt when we do something wrong or make bad decisions. As Charles Curran writes, "Many different criteria have been proposed down through the years, but the most adequate criterion in my judgment is the peace and joy of a good conscience." He continues, "Both the theory and experience of consequent conscience emphasize the remorse of conscience as a sign of an erroneous conscience."[24]

Any person with moral integrity has, on occasion, felt guilty after doing or saying sometime wrong. Some commentators, however, speak of "good" guilt and "bad" guilt. The former has the ability to build us up while the latter can keep us down. We experience negative guilt when we fail to live up to another's standards for us. It is when we do not meet obligations or rules that are placed on us. Good guilt or true guilt stems from something different. The essence of true guilt is the recognition that I have betrayed myself.[25]

You have had these experiences in your own life. You have felt peace or contentment when you did the right thing or after you made a good decision. You have also felt guilt, or you felt "bad" after making poor choices. You also know that at times you are not sure what you feel after a choice. Your feelings are "mixed." Doing the right thing can be hard at times because you may have to choose between two or three goods or goals. A good decision may bring you peace but it may also be troubling and worrisome. For example, you might know deep down that you have to break off a relationship. It is the right thing for you to do at this time, but it is not without tears and sadness.

Conscience as a Voice or Impulse

Most moral decisions you make are quick and impulsive. Perhaps you sense a "voice" inside directing you to do something. Imagine the following scenario: You are walking down a street. As you turn a corner, an elderly woman trips and falls to the ground right in front of you. You probably do not stop to think or reflect on what to do. You act spontaneously (hopefully) to help the woman. You do not think of how this act would benefit you or what universal moral rules you are following. You stop what you are doing and you help the lady. It seems strange to call this a decision, because you acted impulsively or spontaneously. Yet you did make some sort of decision. As you walked down the street, you did not have to stop. History is full of stories of people who see others suffering and stand by and do nothing. When you stopped to help the woman, you were like the Good Samaritan.

Spiritual writer James Martin writes of this time of response: "Occasionally there is no question about what to do." He continues: "One example: You've been searching for a job in a particular city with a particular company, starting at a particular time. After months of interviewing, you land the job. You are elated at your good fortune and sure it is the right move. You accept the new job immediately with barely a thought."[26]

In such cases, a decision, at some level, is made. The point here is that the spontaneous moral decisions you "make" in particular situations are based on previous decisions. For example, if you made the decision to get in shape, you do not deliberate about whether you should go to work out or not. You go work out. If you have made the decision to get good grades, you do not deliberate every night about whether to study or watch television. You study. If you make the decision not to get into arguments with your mother, you do not deliberate every time a conflict arises. If you have made these decisions, a "voice" inside of you reminds you: "Go for a run." "Study now." "Chill out." "Help the old lady on the street who fell down."

You decided not to get into an argument with your mother today based on a previous decision. You decided to help that elderly woman today based on some commitments you made to moral principles or moral goals or to values. Your actions expressed these commitments in a very practical manner. In other words, the actions expressed who you are as a person. Most of our decisions are made on a sense of moral instinct we have, based on the values and moral commitments we have chosen. The impulse or the voice to help another or to direct your behavior in positive ways indicates an active and developing conscience.

This is not to say that all impulsive decisions are appropriate and good. You and I know people who should think things out more clearly before they act (see the next section of this chapter). Quick or impulsive decisions can reflect the person's moral self.

Conscience as a Process

There are times in our lives when we need to stop and think before we act. That is to say, we need to work through a decision. "Should I marry George?" "What should I major in?" "Should I take this job?" These questions are examples of the basic dramatic moral questions people face. The way we answer these questions will give fundamental direction to our lives and will have an impact on our well-being and our relationships.

Judy may want to marry George, while Betty is repelled by the idea. James may enjoy being an accountant, while Johan would find the work frustrating. He would rather be a teacher. The "rightness" or "wrongness" of the answers to these types of questions depends on the person asking the question. The "right" spouse for me is probably very different from the "right" spouse for you. The "right" job or vocation for me is probably different from the "right" job or vocation for you.

Although you may have a different answer to the question, "What is the right job for me?" than I do, there might be strong similarities in the process or the method by which we come to our distinctive decisions. Often when we look back on a particular choice as a bad decision, we find that the process (or perhaps the lack of a process) by which we made the decision to be faulty. How often have you heard someone say to another, "What were you thinking?" All of this is to say that there are better and worse ways to make decisions.

What is a good process or method for making a decision? Most discussions on decision-making follow a process not unlike Thomas Aquinas's reflection on the virtue prudence. "Prudence," according to Aquinas, "is right reason applied to action." He states there are three stages of prudence: "The first act is to take good counsel. It is the process of discovery or inquiry. The second act, an act of speculative reason, is to judge of what one has discovered. The third act regards practical reason. It consists in applying the things discovered and judged to actions."[27] Prudence is "wisdom about human affairs." In simplified language, this process of moral decision-making can be captured in the phrase, "Look, Judge, and Act."

"Looking" demands finding the relevant rules, values, and goods involved in the particular situation. But it is more than that. A good decision, notes Aquinas, requires some memory of the past, a keen understanding of the present, and thoughtful perception of future possibilities. It suggests we have a sense of the consequences of choosing or not choosing. It pushes us to seek advice and be willing to hear the opinions and views of others. Think of the variety of persons who have functioned in your life, either formally or informally, as moral guides or resources. Informally we have been influenced by friends, parents, and family members, as well as by the media and other sources. Formally, teachers and counselors, priests and pastors have influenced us.

A goal of this step is to gain some objectivity, that is to say, to put aside personal preferences and prejudices and look at the situation with clarity. James Martin, following the Ignatian tradition, suggests that an important element of decision-making is "The ability to be detached from one's initial biases and to step back, the willingness to carefully balance the alternatives."[28] One concrete way of doing this is to make a list of pros and cons. Writing things down and putting them in columns can help you gain some objectivity. Martin also recommends using your imagination as well as your intellect here. Imagine yourself living in the possible choices. Imagine the advice you would give another person in a similar position. Imagine yourself in the future, perhaps on your deathbed reflecting on your choice. Imagine "what your best self would do."[29] In short, we must fully "look" at the issue, and its ramifications, clearly.

What one ultimately has to see is how this decision will affect one's relationship to others and to God. That is to say, one must see how this choice will fit into or direct one's sense of calling or vocation in the world. A good decision therefore demands that we turn inside and examine our feelings, senses, and intuitions about the issue at hand. A helpful hint here is to reflect on your state as you make a decision. Are you acting reflectively or are you acting out of a sense of desperation or anger? If this is the case, wait!

After taking counsel and gaining insight from others and honestly examining oneself along with the alternatives and expected outcomes, the person ought to come to a decision about action to be taken in the particular circumstance (I know this perhaps sounds easier than it might really be). This means placing the information learned by "looking" in front of oneself and in conversation with God. The person ought to seek some "space" to be alone. Pray. Ask God for wisdom and the ability to make a good choice.[30]

We cannot underestimate the power of our feelings here. Another way of saying this is that we have to listen to our instincts or, as some people might say, to our "gut." Listen to your instincts. Jesuit spirituality has two words to help us understand our feelings: consolation and desolation. Consolation is "a sense of God's presence" and leads to feelings of "peace, tranquility, and joy." You feel "encouraged and confident, and calm in your decision." Desolation, on the other hand, leads to hopelessness and restlessness, unhappiness, and listlessness.[31]

A few weeks ago I had separate conversations with two colleagues about career choices they were making. Both were leaning toward making particular moves, but to my surprise, they both chose not to make the move and they both gave me the same reason. Each said that the move did not "feel right" for them. They felt a sense of desolation as they reflected on their lives if they were to make the move. All of this is to say that emotions are not simply incidental to our conscience; they are central features to conscience.

All good decisions we make in life are from our heart as well as from our head. They are from our emotional nature as much as they are from our intellect. James Gustafson has it right when he describes the final stage of moral discernment to be "an informed intuition." We do not make good decisions about such choices (for example, to marry or what job or to have children) based on a con-clusion of a clearly argued logical argument. Most of us do not make such judgments on a "strict deduction from a single moral principle, or an absolutely certain result from the exercises of human 'reason' alone." Gustafson says that in a good decision-making process there often is a "moment of perception" when we see things, with our head and our heart, fitting together given the particularities of our lives.[32] We make a decision on *informed* intuition. Kevin O'Rourke seems to agree. He writes, "Intuition, when it is the apprehension of a particular good by an informed conscience, is a legitimate source of a justified moral decision. Christians believe such intuitions are often the result of virtue and the influence of the Holy Spirit. Indeed, it seems that many of the good actions people perform are the result of intuition." In the Christian tradition, "intuition must be supported by principle."[33]

Thus the person judges what he or she thinks is the right thing to do. Yet, a moral decision is not complete until we perform the act or actions we judged to be appropriate. Sometimes this is tough. We must have strength to do what we ought to do. Other times it is easy. The right choice "flows" from us. A person of moral integrity, a person with strong moral identity, is a person who follows his or her "looking" and "judging" with action.[34]

It seems strange to say that "action" is part of conscience, but it is. To fulfill our conscience, we must follow our conscience, either as the impulse to do good or the process of discerning the good. There are several forms moral action can take. The most obvious is interpersonal. Recall the story of the elderly woman who fell down. You stop and help her. But let's say in helping the woman, you notice a contributing factor to her accident. The sidewalk may have been icy or perhaps it was uneven and dangerous. What do you do? Your moral action may take on characteristics beyond the individual one-on-one action. You might complain to the city or the owner of the building where the fall occurred. In other words you respond to a "bigger" problem than the woman falling. You take on moral responsibility to address the cause of the woman falling so it will not happen again to her or to others. If your first action was "interpersonal," your second might be described as "institutional." Let's go further here. You are so taken by this cause of the woman falling, that you notice that all the sidewalks in the area are in disrepair. You also notice that the neighborhood where the senior citizens live is dangerous. Frankly, you realize that there is a social problem with how we treat our seniors. So now what do you do? The moral action of helping the woman who has fallen will no longer suffice. The moral action of making sure the owner of the building shovels the snow will no longer suffice. You must respond to "bigger" problems. You need the community to address the treatment of seniors. You seek community programs, for example, a busing service, to help them. Your moral action is no longer strictly interpersonal nor is it strictly institutional; it is now social.

There are, then, three levels of moral action. It seems as if most people are drawn to one or another type of action. Some of us seem committed to personal, one-on-one actions, and others are driven to work with institutional or social forms of action. Whatever the focus, following one's conscience means acting on one's conscience.

Thomas Aquinas noted something interesting in his discussion of moral action and conscience. Recognizing human weakness, he wrote that a vital part of the virtue that directs conscience is "command." Our reason must "command" us to do what conscience requires.[35] The conscience must, at times, push us to do the right thing at the right time. Underlying Aquinas's thinking here is perhaps the notion that we might not be as free as we think we are in moral affairs (see the notion of "situated freedom" in chapter 2).

This understanding of conscience appears in the Bible, particularly in the writing of St. Paul.[36] Briefly stated, there are several features that stand out in Paul's understanding of conscience. First, conscience is the place in persons for moral judgment and reflection on their past behavior. Thus the author of the Letter to the Hebrews speaks of having a "clear conscience, desiring to act honorably in all things" (Heb. 13:18). Secondly, Paul recognizes conscience as a faculty that all people have. It is not something only believers possess. He writes, "When the Gentiles . . . do instinctively what the law requires . . . they show that what the law requires is written on their hearts, to which their own conscience also bears witness" (Rom. 2:14–15).

Thirdly, Paul realizes that the behavior of some people can influence the conscience of other people. The problem Paul addresses (which is not a problem of our day) is that some Christians were eating meat that had been offered to religious idols. As these Christians did not believe in the reality of these gods, eating food offered to them was not an issue. When other Christians saw them doing this, however, they were scandalized. Paul refers to this second group of Christians as having "weak" consciences. He notes that while eating this type of food was not in itself wrong, it might be a source of scandal to others. Thus he will not eat it (1 Cor. 8:1–13). A conscience can be mistaken and indeed evil; thus it must be perfected and purified (Heb. 9: 9, 14).

The Role of Authority

When Thomas talks about "command" in conscience, he recognizes that at times we have to "force" ourselves to do things. We know we should do something, but at the moment, it seems too demanding or too time consuming. So, he says, we have to tell ourselves to do it (I experience that some mornings. My body does not want to get out of bed, so I have to command myself to get moving!). Aquinas is not talking about being commanded to act by an outside authority here. But this brings up a challenging question. What role ought external authority have on my conscience?

Two truths are in tension at this point. The first is that conscience is personal. Conscience is me coming to a decision for myself. The second is that it is hard to make a good decision, particularly a decision about an important issue, by yourself. You need to talk to someone. You need to consult an authority of some sort.

You must, as Aquinas notes, take counsel from others. For Catholics, the church is a "mother and teacher" of moral truth, the primary source of moral counsel. So then, what role should the church play in a person's decision-making process? If the church has made some declaration on an issue, must the good Catholic follow that decision? This, of course, pertains to major moral issues. The church does not comment on other moral issues, for example, whether you should get married or not. However, the church has authoritatively taught on many issues, including abortion, contraception, embryonic stem cell research, direct euthanasia, capital punishment, just wages, homosexual acts, war, torture, human rights (proclaiming, for example, the right to food, water, health care), immigration, environmental ethics, consumerism, obligations of the better-off to help the lesser-off, the purpose of business, the just workplace and just social order, racism, and so on.

According to the church, Catholics ought to accept these teachings and adhere to them with "religious assent of the soul," or, in other words, with "religious submission of the mind and the will."[37] The U.S. Catholic Bishops write that Catholics ought to recognize the "church's teachings are true and necessary in the formation" of conscience.[38] What if you think, however (against the church), that capital punishment is the appropriate response to a capital crime? What if you think (against the church) that health care is not a right but a privilege, something you earn? What if you come to think (against the church) that homosexual acts or torture or contraception are not always wrong?

We are back to the tension stated above. You have the moral obligation to follow your fully informed conscience. But a fully informed conscience means that you have to know and understand the church teaching. So what do you do if you find yourself in disagreement? You should review your position in light of church teaching and you should presume that the church is right. But what if, after a serious look, you have questions about one or two of the church teachings on moral issues?

Much has been written about Catholics disagreeing with or dissenting from church teaching. It is a complicated issue to be a "loyal dissenter" or to "faithfully disagree" with the church. Some Catholics think there is absolutely no room for dissent. I do not mean to glorify disagreement, but there does seem to be some room here. I think John Mahoney's words are helpful. He writes, "If, then, a person genuinely believes that one line of action rather than another is God's objective expectation of him and that this personal and inalienable moral responsibility lies in this direction then it becomes a matter of saying, not that he is free to follow conscience, but that he is bound to follow conscience."[39]

The voice of conscience comes from within. It may very well espouse the views of an authority, but in the end, it ought to come from personal ownership and responsibility. For, as the church says, "in the depths of conscience" one "is alone with God."[40]

Conscience as a "Place"

We have used the word "heart" often in this book. In our usual conversation, the heart refers to the emotional aspect of a person. This often is used to contrast the "head" or the intellectual aspect of a person. In the Bible, the "heart" refers to the personality of the person. We might say this includes one's emotions as well as one's intellect and will. Thus you are told to "follow your heart" and to "examine your heart." This contemporary metaphorical use of the term is close to the meaning of the term in the Bible.

The word "heart" in the Old Testament is *leb*. According to biblical scholars, *leb* is the "seat of thinking and loving" of a person.[41] In contrast to our contemporary use of the term, which refers exclusively to one's emotional center, the Old Testament uses of the term heart to include the intellectual center of a person. The heart is then where wisdom or good judgment resides. It is the place of thoughtfulness, understanding, and attention.[42]

A few short passages from the Old Testament help give a sense of the meaning of the heart. From the book of Proverbs: "My child, do not forget my teaching, but let your heart keep my commandments. . . . Trust in the LORD with all your heart" (3:1, 5). From Jeremiah: "I will put my law within them, and I will write it on their hearts; and I will be their God, and they shall be my people" (31:33).

Psalm 51:6: "You desire truth in the inward being; therefore teach me wisdom in my secret heart."

The heart is held in high regard in the Bible, but it is not always the source of good judgment and virtue. The heart can be open to God and it can be closed to God. It can be foolish and stubborn, and indeed it can be the source of sin and vice. Isaiah strikingly cites God saying that the people "honor me with their lips, while their hearts are far from me" (29:13). Matthew writes, "Out of the heart comes evil intentions" (Matt. 15:19).

A final passage is from the book of the prophet Hosea. It is interesting here because it speaks of God "following" his heart. The context is that the people have sinned against God and by all rights God should punish them. But he decides he will not because he is God. "My heart recoils within me; my compassion grows warm and tender. I will not execute my fierce anger . . . for I am God and no mortal, the Holy One in your midst, and I will not come in wrath" (Hos. 11:9).

Some have used the word "mind" here to describe the biblical view of the heart.[43] Thus commentators over the years have referred to the "faculty" of conscience. By this they mean that conscience is an ability people are born with. Having a conscience is similar to having other faculties, for example the ability to hear, taste, see, and smell. It is this biblically informed view of the heart, or indeed the conscience, that directs the present work.

But there is more. The idea of the heart includes not only the ability to process thoughts and desires. You experience your "heart" as something of a (metaphorical) "place" within you. The image we have here is the "center" of one's being or personhood. The "place" where you are you and you experience that fundamental power where you can, within your "situated freedom," choose the kind of person you want to be. Your conscience includes the experience of a personal center.

The Catholic Church calls one's conscience a person's "most secret core and sanctuary." "In the depths of conscience" the person "is alone with God."[44] Pope John Paul II wrote that conscience opens a person "to the call, to the voice of God." He then concludes, "In this, and not in anything else, lies the entire mystery and the dignity of the moral conscience: in being the place, the sacred place where God speaks to man."[45] If it is the place where God speaks to us, it is also the place where we can respond to God. It is the "place" where prayer begins. In the words of the *Catechism*, "According to Scripture, it is the heart that prays."[46] The conscience therefore is the place of dialogue with God.[47]

St. Augustine played an important role in describing this feature of the Christian tradition. In his classic book *Confessions,* St. Augustine writes movingly about his path toward God. He examines the world and finds traces and imprints of God, but this is not enough.[48] He then turns inward. The philosopher Charles Taylor describes St. Augustine's journey this way: "God is to be found not just in the world but also and more importantly at the very foundation of the person."[49] For St. Augustine, and indeed for all of us, the "step to inwardness," the reflection on the core of oneself, is "a step toward God."[50] As Taylor notes, "By going inward, I am drawn upward."[51] This is somewhat hard to describe because the sense of "going within oneself to a place" leads to the realization that the truth is not really in me. What is in me is the "place" to encounter what the truth is. In Taylor's words, "I see the truth 'in' God."[52]

In order to fully experience this core, this sacred place within, a person must be "sufficiently present" to oneself. That is to say, the person must have a sense of interiority and a level of self-reflection and self-examination.[53] This takes some effort. It is a practice that is in some sense counter to our basic cultural practices. It is not a stretch to say that all writers on the spiritual life note the importance of quietness and stillness in one's life. Consider the following quotation written in 1965 by Thomas Merton: "Now let us frankly face the fact that our culture is one which is geared in many ways to help us evade any need to face this inner, silent self. We live in a state of constant semi-attention to the sound of voices, music, traffic, or the generalized noise of what goes on around us all the time. . . . All of this can be described as 'noise,' as commotion and jamming which drown out the deep, secret, and insistent demands of the inner self."[54] That was 1965; the "noise" is so much louder today!

Like Merton, and indeed all people who write on the spiritual life, Blessed Mother Teresa noted the importance of reflection and silence to hear God. "If we really want to pray we must first learn to listen, for in the silence of the heart God speaks. And to be able to hear that silence, to be able to hear God we need a clean heart, for a clean heart can see God, can hear God, can listen to God, and then only from the fullness of our heart can we speak to God. But we cannot speak unless we have listened, unless we have made that connection with God in the silence of our heart."[55]

The contemporary spiritual writer James Martin writes, "We are gradually losing the art of silence. Of walking down the street lost in our own thoughts. Of closing the door to our rooms and being quiet. Of sitting on a park bench and just thinking. We may fear silence because we fear what we might hear from the deepest part of ourselves."[56]

Martin encourages people to consider the simple and time-honored spiritual practice of the Jesuits (his religious order). It is an examination of one's conscience in prayer every day. The process, called the "examen," has five steps. The first step is simply to express gratitude to God. You should begin your daily examination of conscience by giving thanks to God for the good and the grace you have received that day and indeed in your life. In the second step, you review your day and recall your experiences of goodness and of God. You should also review your experiences of sin and moral shortcomings. Third, you should "own-up-to" your shortcomings and recognize things for which you are sorry. Fourth, you ask God for forgiveness. If you hurt anyone, you should reflect on how you might begin to repair the relationship. Fifth, you ask God for the grace to grow beyond your shortcomings and resolve to see God more clearly in the coming day.[57] The examen is simple and easy; it can be done in a few minutes. But it can also be life-directing.

Martin's thoughts here point to a deeper issue. You and I need to engage in spiritual practices that provide structured opportunities for reflection. Traditional spirituality calls us to three such practices: almsgiving, prayer, and fasting. All of these are external actions based on internal dispositions. Jesus refers to these in the Sermon on the Mount. Recall that he pushes his listeners to reflect on their intentions as they practice these actions. When you give alms, he said, "do not let your left hand know what your right hand is doing" (Matt. 6:3). When you pray, "go into your room and shut the door" (Matt. 6:6). When you fast, "put oil on your head and wash your face [that is to say, make yourself look good so others do not know you are fasting]" (Matt. 6:17). These practices have moral implications. But there is more. When we give alms, pray, and fast with our hearts open to the Spirit of Jesus, we are invited and indeed challenged (even "forced") to examine ourselves.[58]

Here is the message of this section: We all have a "secret core and sanctuary," yet not all of us take the time to leave the noise of every-day life to find this core. To quote the psalmist, "Be still, and know that I am God!" (Ps. 46:10). I do not have any empirical evidence on this, but it is my guess that people who take some time to reflect on their lives are probably more likely to make good decisions in their lives. A prerequisite for making a good decision next year might be the practice of moral and spiritual reflection today and tomorrow.

The description of this part of conscience here so far has been explicitly religious. One can think of, however, nontheological ways in which to describe this. If the argument here is correct and all peo-ple, religious or not, have a conscience, then nonreligious people would experience this feature of conscience differently than reli-gious people. They would not say, for example, that conscience is where God speaks to them or where they meet God. Yet they might say that they experience some personal "center" of value or they sense a "core" of their being. They might describe this "place" as their heart where they hear the moral call.

This discussion between the believer and nonbeliever might give us some pause. Perhaps the language of the preceding para-graphs is too religious. Perhaps the descriptions of this part of con-science overstate what most of us experience. Many believers might not explicitly say that they have heard God in their hearts. Their experience of God might be fuzzy, vague, and inarticulate.[59] The fun-damental point here is that the elementary experience of conscience is as "place" within us. "It is a place of encounter" because we are persons in relation to others and to God.[60] Only secondarily then is the conscience a place of decision. Conscience or "with knowledge" refers to the fundamental sense of the "center" of oneself.

In an opening quotation of this chapter, St. Paul calls the Corinthians to "examine" and "test" themselves. The conscience is that place where we do that. It is the place for us to reflect on the particular feelings we have as a result of our actions. It is the place to grow sympathy into empathy into compassion and perhaps into solidarity. It is the place to recall our impulsive actions and why we did them. It is also the place to review our decision-making processes.

The conscience is where one "hears" the call to be moral before one processes morality. It is where the subjective self meets the objective. The conscience is where one takes rules, goods, and virtues "to heart." It is also the place where one rejects or ignores the rules, goods, and virtues. The objective or communal nature of morality appeals fundamentally to the first part of conscience, thus the notion that this is "a place of encounter."

Conscience of a Community

Anyone who has seen the classic 1940 Disney movie *Pinocchio* has also seen a classic depiction of conscience. In the film, a woodcrafter named Geppetto makes a puppet, Pinocchio, out of wood. Geppetto wishes the puppet would become a real boy, and one night the Blue Fairy comes to his house and partially answers his wish. She brings Pinocchio to life, but he is basically a walking and talking puppet, not a human. Pinocchio must earn personhood, she says, by acting "brave, truthful, and unselfish." This is not an easy task. The Blue Fairy knows this and appoints a cricket named Jiminy to be Pinocchio's "conscience." For how can one achieve full personhood without a conscience?

The movie is about Pinocchio's trials and tribulations on the way to personhood. With Jiminy's help, the puppet achieves his goal. Once Pinocchio becomes a boy, Jiminy's job is complete (and the Blue Fairy awards him a badge of conscience). Pinocchio, now a person, has his own internal conscience. (In the original 1881 story, the cricket kills Pinocchio for all his moral advice!)

The film is a "classic" but not just because it is old and cute. It is a classic because in its simplistic, childish way, it reminds us that there are times when we "lose" our humanness and we too need a Jiminy Cricket. We need someone who (metaphorically) stands outside or above us and has the vocation (literally) to get our attention to tell us the truth. While we all have interior consciences, we are often in need of persons who function like consciences in society.

The Bible is full of people who were like consciences for their communities. They are called prophets. The Old Testament names over fifty people as prophets, including Sarah, Moses, Miriam, Isaiah, Amos, Hosea, and Micah. These people often used strong and impassioned language to "awaken" their people to the reality of their lives. The people, individuals and groups, were engaged in what they generally thought of as "normal" behavior for their culture. The prophets condemned this socially acceptable behavior and called the people to higher moral and religious ground. The prophet Isaiah, for example, strongly criticized the ruling class of his time for, among other things, taking bribes and creating unjust laws that robbed and crushed the poor (see Isa. 1:21–23; 3:14–15; 10:1–2). Amos condemned the rich for trampling on "the heads of the poor" (Amos 2:6–7). Micah indicted the leaders as well as the sellers of goods in the marketplace for stealing from and lying to the poor (Mic. 2:2; 6:9–12). Just as Isaiah, Amos, and Micah saw the social evil and condemned it eight hundred years before Jesus, Martin Luther King Jr. saw social evil and condemned it nineteen hundred years after Jesus. Racism, prejudice, and segregation laws were all part of the "normal" and socially acceptable culture of America. King saw this, named this, and called the community to higher moral ground. The torture and killing of Jews in Nazi laboratories was "normal" and socially acceptable behavior. Elie Wiesel has committed his life to the cause of never allowing that behavior be "normal" again.

After their critique of social ills, prophets challenge the people to live moral lives and to build a moral future. Isaiah boldly proclaims that the people will "beat their swords into plowshares and their spears into pruning hooks; nations shall not lift up sword against nations, neither shall they learn war any more" (2:4). Micah concludes, "He has told you, O mortal, what is good; and what does the Lord require of you but to do justice, and to love kindness, and to walk humbly with your God" (6:8).

Prophets are like consciences for communities. First, they are moral voices calling people to higher moral ground. Second, they demand that you stop and think about your behavior and your attitudes. You should process what you are doing. Third, they spark emotions, often anger (look what is happening!) or guilt (are you allowing this to happen?), but also hope (we can change this!). They do all this so as to incite moral growth and change.

Moral Identity

Conscience refers to the *source of feelings* that spring up in us as a consequence of our actions. It also refers to the reflective *process* of working through a decision. Conscience is that *place* within us; and it refers to the strong sense, or *voice*, we have at times directing us to do or not do something. We subjectively experience these aspects of conscience, but at times we are so caught up in workings of culture and life that we need people to act like a conscience for our communities. Perhaps there may be times when you need to act as a conscience for one of your communities.

We end with three principles of conscience:

1. You have the moral responsibility to *follow* your conscience;

2. You have the moral responsibility *to develop* your conscience; and

3. You have the moral responsibility to *respect* the conscience of others.

You have the moral responsibility to follow your conscience. If you have honestly and faithfully examined your conscience, you ought to act accordingly. You ought to be the person your conscience tells you to be. Commentators on conscience are often quick to note here that although you ought to follow your conscience, you can and do make mistakes. Honest people "mess up." Good people disagree about the right thing to do. At issue here is moral integrity or what we have been calling moral identity rather than a question of

moral perfection. Moral identity is not simply a question of appropriate feelings or of knowing the right and the good. It is a question
of how those feelings and knowledge lead you to do the right thing
and to be a good person.

You have the moral responsibility to develop your conscience.
A developing conscience needs a sense of objectivity along with a
growing ability to see others as persons. At the base of conscience
are two sets of feelings. The first is feeling for others in their joys and
sufferings. The second is feeling when our actions affect another.
This chapter has suggested that we need to push these feelings into
action through compassion and perhaps even through solidarity.
The developing conscience embraces these feelings and to them it
adds the ability to deliberate and to make choices. Along with compassion, we need a strong sense of human rights, appropriate sense
of rules, the proper intentions/goals, and, of course, virtues.

To do this well, we need to nurture the "space" within ourselves.
A developing conscience knows that it is not simply "about me."
Recall the biblical warnings that one's conscience can indeed be
foolish and stubborn. It can be weak, mistaken, and selfish. We can
close our "hearts" to God and to others. The maturing conscience
overcomes "fear, selfishness, and pride, resentment arising from
guilt, and feelings of complacency, born of human weakness and
faults."[61] The maturing conscience leads to a deeper sense of the self
as a free person.

You have the moral responsibility to respect the conscience of
others. As your conscience is your "secret core and sanctuary," so it
is with your neighbor. In conscience you experience your freedoms
and your responsibilities; so it is with your neighbor. Conscience is a
place were your feelings and intuitions meet reason, clear thinking,
and the basic elements of morality; so it is with your neighbor.

Questions

1. Which feature of conscience ought to be the most important in a person's life? Explain your thinking.

2. Do you think these features of conscience develop as one grows? That is to say, do these features change as one moves from childhood through adolescence and through emerging adulthood into adulthood? Explain your thinking.

3. If there are mistaken views of conscience in general, are there mistaken views of the features of conscience? What might they be? Explain your thinking.

4. Using elements from this chapter explain the concept of moral identity.

CONCLUSION

The Moral of This Story Is . . .

The joys and the hopes, the griefs and the anxieties of the people of this age, especially those who are poor or in any way afflicted, these are the joys and hopes, the griefs and anxieties of the followers of Christ. —Second Vatican Council, *Gaudium et Spes*

Teacher, which commandment in the law is the greatest? And he said to him, "You shall love the Lord your God with all your heart, and with all your soul, and with all your mind." This is the greatest and first commandment. And a second is like it: "You shall love your neighbor as yourself." —Matthew 22:36–40

The moral of this story is that people talk about morality in at least four different ways: through story (narrative), through passionate language (prophetic), through reasoned argument (ethics), and through seeking pragmatic practices (policy). One of these fits you more than the others. Own it. Just do not forget that some day you will be called, by your own sense of moral identity, to speak adequately within each of the other three voices.

The moral of this story is that an essential feature of your moral personhood is the complex experiences of freedom you have (freedom from the interference of others, freedom for simple goods, freedom for complex goods, and the freedom within your "heart"). When you think about these experiences over time you will sense a direction in your life. You will have to decide whether or not the direction is your choice.

The moral of this story is that four sets of moral ideas direct your life (rights, rules, intentions/goals, and virtues). Like the man and woman in Genesis 1–3; the priest, the Levite, and the Samaritan; and Mary and Martha, you have the burden and the joy of determining which rights you will respect in others, which rules will direct your life, which intentions and goals will inspire you, and which virtues you will hold to define your life. Moral theology, after all, exists "outside" of you. Your moral identity is defined by what you let in.

The moral of this story is that sometime in the near future you ought to take the time and "peel away" at your moral identity. Think about a choice you recently made, a choice that has some ramifications for your life (for example, something you did with a friend or friends, or a choice related to your future). Think about why you made that choice. Would you make that choice again tomorrow? What does that choice say about you as a person? Go deeper. What do you find in your heart about the beliefs or commitments you have? Do you have any such depth?

The moral of this story is that the greatest rule in life, the most significant intention/goal in life, and the highest virtue in life is to love *what* God loves ("God loves God, the world, other persons, and me") and to love *how* God loves (with strong emotions, in a way that affirms the other, is responsive to the reality of the other, and that bonds you to the other in an enduring way). To do so is to become the seed or the leaven for the kingdom that we pray will come "on earth as it is in heaven."

The moral of this story is that your particular day-in and day-out actions are expressions of who you are as a person (acts and intentions within circumstances) at that particular moment and that through such actions you are creating and sustaining your moral identity and life narrative.

The moral of this story is that you are a thinking, feeling person who is related to others in multiple ways. Your moral voice, your freedom, your set of moral ideas, your call to love, and the direction of your life narrative all come together in your conscience. Nourish your secret core and sanctuary. Honestly think through decisions. Listen to your deep feelings. Respond to the voice of love within.

Notes

Introduction

1. G. K. Chesterton, *The Catholic Church and Conversion* (San Francisco: Ignatius Press, 1990), 38.

2. My colleague Tonia Bock introduced the idea of moral identity to me in her essay, "Are You a Good Person?" *Spotlight* (University of St. Thomas College of Arts and Sciences Magazine): 5, no. 2 (Spring 2013): 16–17. For an overview of the idea of moral identity in psychology, see Sam Hardy and Gustavo Carlo, "Moral Identity: What Is It, How Does It Develop, and Is It Linked to Moral Action?" *Child Development Perspectives* 5 (2011): 212–18; and Darcia Narvaez and Daniel Lapsley, "Moral Identity, Moral Functioning, and the Development of Moral Character," *Psychology of Learning and Motivation* 50 (2009): 237–74.

3. Bock, "Are You a Good Person?" 17.

4. Hardy and Carlo, "Moral Identity," 213.

5. Ibid.

Chapter 1: How People Talk about Morality

1. Gerhard Lohfink, *Jesus of Nazareth: What He Wanted, Who He Was* (Collegeville, MN: Michael Glazier Books, 2012), 102.

2. Richard Clifford and Roland Murphy, "Genesis," in *The New Jerome Biblical Commentary*, ed. Raymond Brown, Joseph Fitzmyer, Roland Murphy (Englewood Cliffs, NJ: Prentice Hall, 1990), 9.

3. Some scholars argue for a unity between the two chapters while admitting different authors. See, for example, E. A. Speiser, *Genesis: Introduction, Translation and Notes, The Anchor Bible*, vol. 1 (Garden City, NY: Doubleday, 1964), 18. Others argue that these are two of the five "self-contained accounts of creation in the OT." William Brown, "Biblical Accounts of Creation," in *Dictionary of Scripture and Ethics*, ed. Joel Green (Grand Rapids, MI: Baker Academic, 2011), 187. The others are: Job 38–41, Psalm 104, and Proverbs 8:22–31. Brown also cites Ecclesiastes 1:3–11, Isaiah 40–55 and John 1:1–18 as biblical texts that describe creation.

4. On this text, Pope Benedict writes, "But the true meaning of God's original command, as the Book of Genesis clearly shows, was not a simple conferral of authority, but rather a summons to responsibility." Pope Benedict XVI, "If You Want to Cultivate Peace, Protect Creation: World Day of

Peace, January 1, 2010," no. 6. According to The Pontifical Biblical Commission, "The guidance entrusted to human beings implies responsibility, the commitment to govern and administer. They have also the duty to give shape in a creative way to the world made by God." Pontifical Biblical Commission, *The Bible and Morality: Biblical Roots of Christian Conduct*, no. 11. See also William Brown, "Biblical Accounts of Creation," 191, and Terence E. Fretheim, "The Book of Genesis," in *The New Interpreter's Bible: Old Testament Survey* (Nashville: Abingdon Press, 2005).

5. Fretheim, "The Book of Genesis," 346.

6. Leslie Marmon Siko, *Ceremony* (New York: Penguin Books, 1977), 2.

7. Benedict Viviano, "The Gospel According to Matthew," in *The New Jerome Biblical Commentary*, ed. Raymond Brown, Joseph Fitzmeyer, Roland Murphy (Englewood Cliffs, NJ: Prentice Hall, 1990), 642.

8. Martin Luther King Jr., "I Have a Dream," in *I Have a Dream: Writings and Speeches That Changed the World,* ed. James Washington (New York: Harper Collins, 1992), 102.

9. Ibid., 103–4.

10. Ibid., 104.

11. Ibid., 106.

12. Augustine, *Tractates on the First Epistle of John*, trans. John Rettig, Tractates on the Gospel of John 112–24 (Washington, DC: Catholic University of America Press, 1995), 7.8, 223.

13. Augustine, "Sermon 344," in *The Works of Saint Augustine: A Translation for the 21st Century, Sermons III/10 (341–400) on Various Subjects,* ed. John Rotelle (Hyde Park, NY: New City Press, 1995), 49.

14. See Michael Perry, *Love and Power: The Role of Religion and Morality in American Politics* (New York: Oxford University Press, 1991), 105.

15. Ibid., 290.

16. Martin Luther King Jr., "Letter from Birmingham City Jail," in *A Testament of Hope: The Essential Writings and Speeches of Martin Luther King Jr.,* ed. James Washington (San Franciso: HarperSanFranciso, 1991), 293.

17. Ibid., 294.

18. this is a simplistic take on Laurence Kohlberg's stages of moral development. See William Crain, *Theories of Development* (Upper Saddle River, NJ: Prentice-Hall, 2000), 149–56.

19. Pontifical Biblical Commission, *The Bible and Morality*, no. 138.

20. http://www.stthomas.edu/media/studentpolicies.

21. http://www.state.gov/s/ocr/c14800.htm.

22. Cathleen Kaveny, *Law's Virtues: Fostering Autonomy and Solidarity in American Society* (Washington, DC: Georgetown University Press, 2012), 45.

23. Thomas Aquinas, *Summa theologica* (New York: Benziger Brothers, 1947), 90.4.

24. Ibid., 95.2.

25. Ibid.

26. Ibid., 96.2.

27. Ibid.

28. Ibid., 95.3.

29. Murray, *We Hold These Truths* (Kansas City, MO: Sheed and Ward, 1960), 272.

30. Ibid., 166.

31. Ibid.

32. National Conference of Catholic Bishops, *Economic Justice for All*, in *Catholic Social Thought: The Documentary Heritage,* ed. David O'Brien and Thomas Shannon (Maryknoll, NY: Orbis Books, 2010), 134.

33. Ibid.

34. See Kaveny, *Law's Virtues,* chapter 2.

35. King, *I Have a Dream,* 25.

36. For an excellent video on these events see Judith Vecchione, Orlando Bagwell, James DeVinney, Callie Crossley, Henry Hampton, Jon Else, Mark Samels, Steve Fayer, and Julian Bond, *Eyes on the Prize: America's Civil Rights Years* (Boston: PBS Distribution, 2010), Disk 2: "No Easy Walk, 1961–1963."

37. David Oppenheimer, "Dr. King's Legal Legacy: A Critical Analysis," 33 *Deutsch-Amerikanische Juristen-Vereinigung Newsletter,* 31 (2008).

38. Ibid., 31–32.

39. See James Gustafson, *A Sense of the Divine: The Natural Environment from a Theocentric Perspective* (Cleveland: Pilgrim Press, 1994).

Chapter 2: Freedom and Expectations

1. Maya Angelou, *The Complete Collected Poems of Maya Angelou* (New York: Random House, 1994), 195. Katie Moore, former graduate student of mine, pointed this poem out to me as a powerful expression of the experience of freedom.

2. This view of freedom is dependent on the classic article by Gerald MacCallum. See Gerald MacCallum, "Negative and Positive Freedom," *The Philosophical Review* 76, no. 3 (July 1967): 312–34. See also Ian Carter,

"Positive and Negative Liberty," in *Stanford Encyclopedia of Philosophy* (Fall 2008 Edition), http://plato.stanford.edu.

3. Second Vatican Council, *Gaudium et Spes,* no. 31.

4. See Cathleen Kaveny, *Law's Virtues: Fostering Autonomy and Solidarity in American Society* (Washington, DC: Georgetown University Press, 2012), chapter 1.

5. *Catechism of the Catholic Church*, no. 2563.

6. John Mahoney, *The Making of Moral Theology: A Study of the Roman Catholic Tradition* (Oxford: Clarendon Press, 1989), 221.

7. Charles Curran, *Catholic Moral Theology in the United States: A History* (Washington, DC: Georgetown University Press, 2008), 171.

8. Margaret Farley, *Personal Commitments: Beginning, Keeping, Changing* (San Francisco: Harper & Row, 1986), 105.

9. Ibid., 106 (emphasis added). This seems to be another way of stating the traditional notion that one cannot sin for the good of another. See Thomas Aquinas, *Summa Theologica* (New York: Benziger Brothers, 1947), II–I, 26.4.

10. See Robert Schreiter, "A Practical Theology of Healing, Forgiveness, and Reconciliation," in *Peacebuilding: Catholic Theology, Ethics and Praxis,* ed. Robert Schreiter, R. Scott Appleby, Gerald Powers (Maryknoll, NY: Orbis Books, 2010), 391.

11. Second Vatican Council, *Dignitatis Humanae*, no. 10.

12. Michael Lawler, "Marriage and the Sacrament of Marriage," in *Christian Marriage and Family: Contemporary Theological and Pastoral Perspectives,* ed. Michael Lawler and William Roberts (Collegeville, MN: Liturgical Press, 1996), 28.

13. Viktor Frankl, *Man's Search for Meaning: An Introduction to Logotheraphy* (New York: Simon & Schuster, 1984), 47.

14. Ibid., 74–75.

15. National Institute on Drug Abuse, *Drugs, Brains, and Behavior: The Science of Addiction*, http://www.drugabuse.gov. Published August 2010.

16. Augustine, *Confessions,* trans. Henry Chadwick (New York: Oxford University Press, 1991), 45.

17. Pope John XXIII, *Pacem in Terris*, nos. 9–27. This section from *Pacem in Terris* is abridged and the use of "man" and "he" in the original was changed to "person." This text is found in Bernard Brady, *Essential Catholic Social Thought* (Maryknoll, NY: Orbis, 2008), 95–96.

18. Pontifical Council for Justice and Peace, *Compendium of the Social Doctrine of the Church*, no. 153. Emphasis is in the original text.

19. The listing of the Ten Commandments here follows the Roman Catholic and Lutheran presentation. Some Protestant denominations present the numbering differently. They break the first one into two and combine the last two into one.

20. See also Mark 12:28–34 and Luke 10:25–28.

21. Thomas Aquinas, *Summa Theologica*, I–II, Q. 94, Art. 2.

22. John Mahoney, *The Making of Moral Theology: A Study of the Roman Catholic Tradition* (Oxford: Clarendon Press, 1989), 258.

23. Charles Taylor, *A Secular Age* (Cambridge, MA: Belknap Press of Harvard University Press, 2007), 704.

24. Ibid.

25. Ibid.

26. Richard Gula, *Reason Informed by Faith* (Mahwah, NJ: Paulist Press, 1989), 265.

27. See Aristotle, *The Nicomachean Ethics* (Oxford: Oxford University Press, 1991), Book 6, 2:38.

28. Pontifical Council for Justice and Peace, *Compendium of the Social Doctrine of the Church*, no. 192.

29. Ibid., no.193.

30. Ibid., no.196.

31. Ibid., no. 193.

32. Ibid.

33. See Thomas Aquinas, *Summa Theologica*, Q. 58, Art. 1.

34. Jean Porter, *The Recovery of Virtue: The Relevance of Aquinas for Christian Ethics* (Louisville: Westminster/John Knox, 1990), 70.

35. See Character Education Partnership, "11 Principles of Effective Character Education" (Washington, DC: Character Education Partnership, 2010).

36. See Malcolm Gladwell, *Outliers: The Story of Success* (New York: Little, Brown and Company, 2008).

37. Character Education Partnership, "11 Principles of Effective Character Education," 2.

38. James Gustafson, *Can Ethics Be Christian?* (Chicago: University of Chicago Press, 1975), 27.

39. Ibid., 47.

40. James Gustafson, Thoe Boer, and Paul Capetz, eds., *Moral Discernment in the Christian Life* (Louisville: Westminster John Knox Press, 2007), 87.

41. Ibid., 88.

42. Richard Gula, *Just Ministry: Professional Ethics for Pastoral Ministers* (New York: Paulist Press, 2010), 67.

Chapter 3: Relationality and Love

1. Martin Luther King Jr., James Washington, ed., *A Testament of Hope: Essential Writings of Martin Luther King Jr.* (San Francisco: HarperCollins, 1986), 19.

2. Paul VI, *Octogesima Adveniens*, no. 4.

3. John XXIII, *Mater et Magistra*, no. 263.

4. John O'Malley describes *Gaudium et Spes* as "the most distinctive" document produced by the Council and "the one perhaps most revelatory of the council's meaning." *What Happened at Vatican II* (Cambridge: The Belknap Press of Harvard University Press, 2008), 158. Eric Borgman described *Gaudium et Spes* as the "epitome" of the council. Eric Borgman, "*Gaudium et Spes*: The Forgotten Future of a Revolutionary Document," in *Vatican II: A Forgotten Future*, ed. Alberto Melloni and Christoph Theobald (London: SCM Press, 2005), 48. This document has had and continues to have an enormous impact on Catholic morality. For example, Joseph Selling writes, "I suggest that, as far as the discipline of moral theology is concerned, the teaching of *Gaudium et Spes* has become normative in the contemporary church. It is the benchmark for the state of the art and is ignored only at one's professional peril." Joseph Selling, "*Gaudium et Spes*: A Manifesto for Contemporary Moral Theology," in *Vatican II and Its Legacy*, ed. M. Lamberigts and L. Kenis (Leuven, Belgium: Leuven University Press, 2002), 152. David Hollenbach writes: "Overall, it can be regarded as the most authoritative and significant document of Catholic social teaching issued in the twentieth century." David Hollenbach, "Commentary on *Gaudium et Spes*," in *Modern Catholic Social Teaching: Commentaries & Interpretations*, ed. Kenneth Himes (Washington, DC: Georgetown University Press, 2005), 266.

5. The Council was, in the words of Church historian John O'Malley, the "biggest meeting in the history of the world." O'Malley, *What Happened at Vatican II*, 295. Moralist John Mahoney described it as "the most momentous exercise to date of the Church's hierarchical magisterium in all its history." John Mahoney, *The Making of Moral Theology: A Study of the Roman Catholic Tradition* (Oxford: Clarendon Press, 1989), 302.

6. Pope John Paul II links this paragraph to his "personalistic principle." See John Paul II, *Crossing the Threshold of Hope* (New York: Albert A. Knopf, 1994), 200–202. For more on what "personalism" means for the pope, see Janet Smith, "Natural Law and Personalism in *Veritatis Splendor*,"

in Charles Curran and Richard McCormick, *John Paul II and Moral Theology: Readings in Moral Theology*, no. 10 (New York: Paulist Press, 1998).

7. Note that the words "Theology," "Anthropology," "Morality" and "Appropriation" do not appear in the original text. Note also that two sentences in the original text were moved to fit into the categories.

8. Commenting on this Paragraph 24's use of Genesis, Otto Semmelroth writes, "This is intended to stress that different though men and woman are, they are both in God's image. Consequently no other difference, racial, national, or individual can destroy this fundamental community of likeness to God." There is then, "an essential community which links men together in a family and demands a fraternal spirit between them." Semmelroth, "Part I, Chapter II, The Community of Mankind," in *Commentary on the Documents of Vatican II*, vol. 5, ed. Herbert Vorgrimler (New York: Herder and Herder, 1969), 166.

9. Pontifical Biblical Commission, *The Bible and Morality: Biblical Roots of Christian Conduct*, no. 42.

10. Gerhard Lohfink, *Jesus of Nazareth: What He Wanted, Who He Was* (Collegeville, MN: Liturgical Press, 2012), 348. Lohfink notes that most biblical translations use "kingdom" rather than "reign." While he suggests reign is preferable, he uses kingdom throughout his discussion. See pages 24–26.

11. Richard Hays, *The Moral Vision of the New Testament* (New York: HarperCollins Publishers Inc., 1996), 127.

12. Lohfink, *Jesus of Nazareth,* 356.

13. Ibid., 39.

14. John Paul II, *Sollicitudo Rei Socialis.*

15. Ibid., 64.

16. Richard Gula, *Reason Informed by Faith* (New York: Paulist Press, 1989), 174.

17. Lohfink, *Jesus of Nazareth,* 32.

18. Francis, *Evangelii Gaudium,* no. 278.

19. Pontifical Biblical Commission, *The Bible and Morality*, no. 42.

20. Lohfink, *Jesus of Nazareth,* 52. See pages 50–52 for a broader discussion of Luke 17:21.

21. Francis, *Evangelii Gaudium,* no. 180.

22. Pontifical Biblical Commission, *The Bible and Morality*, no. 43.

23. Lohfink, *Jesus of Nazareth,* 51.

24. Pontifical Biblical Commission, *The Bible and Morality*, no. 158.

25. Gary Anderson, *Charity: The Place of the Poor in the Biblical Tradition* (New Haven: Yale University Press, 2013), 4.

26. Ibid., 7–8. I am taking this beyond Anderson's intent. His argument concerns charity, that is, monetary gifts.

27. Francis, *Evangelii Gaudium*, no. 225.

28. Ibid., 197.

29. Pontifical Biblical Commission, *The Bible and Morality*, no. 121.

30. Ibid., 224–25.

31. Ibid., 141.

32. Martha Nussbaum, *The Fragility of Goodness: Luck and Ethics in Greek Tragedy and Philosophy* (Cambridge: Cambridge University Press, 1986), 1.

33. Ibid.

34. Ibid.

35. Ibid.

36. Edward Vacek, *Love, Human and Divine: The Heart of Christian Ethics* (Washington, DC: Georgetown, 1994), 298.

37. Cathleen Kaveny, 79.

38. Joseph Ratzinger, *On Conscience* (San Francisco: Ignatius Press, 2007), 53.

39. Pontifical Council for Justice and Peace, *Compendium of the Social Doctrine of the Church,* no. 164.

40. Ibid., no. 165.

41. John Paul II, *Sollicitudo Rei Socialis*, no. 38.

42. Ibid., no. 40.

43. www.thekingcenter.org/king-philosophy.

44. Pontifical Biblical Commission, *The Bible and Morality*, no. 118.

45. Francis, *Evangelii Gaudium*, nos. 222–23.

46. Pontifical Biblical Commission, *The Bible and Morality*, no. 131.

47. Ibid., no. 138.

48. Ibid., no. 148.

49. Ibid., no. 158.

50. See, for example, Massingale, *Racial Justice and the Catholic Church,* 78,104–11,130–40; Diana Hayes, *Forged in the Fiery Furnace: African American Spirituality* (Maryknoll, NY: Orbis Books, 2012), 69–87; James Cone, *The Cross and the Lynching Tree* (Maryknoll, NY: Orbis Books, 2011), 1–29; and Thea Bowman, "The Gift of African American Sacred Song," *Lead Me, Guide Me: The African American Catholic Hymnal* (Chicago: G.I.A. Publications, 1987).

51. Massingale, *Racial Justice and the Catholic Church,* 148.

52. Michael Coogan, ed., *The New Oxford Annotated Bible* (NRSV) (Oxford: Oxford University Press, 2001), 118 in the New Testament.

53. Michel Gourgues, "The Priest, the Levite, and the Samaritan Revisited: A Critical Note on Luke 10:31-35," *Journal of Biblical Literature* 117, no. 4 (1998), questions this reading, noting that the men were "not on their way up to Jerusalem but on their way back," 709.

54. Ibid., 710.

55. See Bruce Longenecker, "The Story of the Samaritan and the Innkeeper (Luke 10:30-35): A Study in Character Rehabilitation," *Biblical Interpretation* 17 (2009): 422-47.

56. Ibid., 446-47.

57. Amartya Sen, *The Idea of Justice* (Cambridge, MA: Belknap Press of Harvard University Press, 2009), 172.

58. Ibid., 173.

59. Robert Karris, "The Gospel According to Luke," in *The New Jerome Biblical Commentary,* ed. Raymond Brown, Joseph Fitzmyer, Roland Murphy (Englewood Cliffs, NJ: Prentice Hall, 1990), 702.

60. Stephen Pope, *Human Evolution and Christian Ethics* (Cambridge: Cambridge University Press, 2007), 245.

61. Ibid., 246.

62. Allen Verhey, *The Great Reversal: Ethics and the New Testament* (Grand Rapids, MI: William Eerdmans, 1984), 19.

63. John Donahue, *The Gospel in Parable* (Philadelphia: Fortress Press, 1988), 136-37.

64. See Paul Hammer, "Inheritence," *The Anchor Bible Dictionary*, vol. 3, 1992, 416.

65. H. Richard Niebuhr, *The Responsible Self* (San Francisco: Harper & Row, 1963), 67. This paragraph is informed by this book.

66. Pope Francis, *Lumen Fidei*, no. 18.

67. James Gustafson, *Can Ethics Be Christian?* (Chicago: University of Chicago Press, 1975), 175.

68. See Augustine, *The Trinity*, trans. Stephen McKenna (Washington, DC: Catholic University Press of America, 1963) Book 8, chap. 10, 266, and Thomas Aquinas, *Summa Theologica* (New York: Benziger Brothers, 1947), I-II, Q. 28.

69. Vacek, *Love, Human and Divine*, 149 (italics added).

70. This view is from Catholic moral theology on love. See Farley, *Personal Commitments*; Vacek, *Love, Human and Divine*; and, Bernard Brady,

Christian Love (Washington, DC: Georgetown University Press, 2003), chapter 11.

71. See, for example, Thomas Aquinas, *Summa Theologica*, I-II, Q. 25.

72. Benedict XVI, *Deus caritas est*, no. 34.

73. Jules Toner, *The Experience of Love* (Washington: Corpus Books, 1968), p. 127.

74. Thomas describes three stages in charity. Beginners work to avoid sin. In the second stage, persons aim to be and do good. The perfection of charity is "union with and enjoyment of God." Thomas Aquinas, *Summa Theologica*, II-II, Q. 24, Art. 9.

75. Benedict XVI, *Deus caritas est*, no. 6.

76. Ibid.

77. Augustine, *On Christian Doctrine*, trans. D. W. Robertson (Indianapolis: Bobbs-Merrill Company, 1958), Book I, chapter 26, 23.

78. Ibid., Book 1, chapter 22, 18–19.

79. Augustine, *On the Morals of the Catholic Church, The Nicene and Post-Nicene Fathers of the Christian Church, Vol. IV: St. Augustine: The Writing Against the Manicheans and Against the Donatists,* ed. Philip Schaff (Grand Rapids, MI: Wm. B. Eerdmans, 1983), chap. 26, 55.

80. Augustine, *The Trinity,* trans. Stephen McKenna (Washington, DC: Catholic University Press of America, 1963), Book 14, chap. 14, 435–36.

81. Augustine, *On Christian Doctrine,* Book I, chap. 32, 19–20.

82. Bernard of Clairvaux, *On Loving God,* trans. Emero Steigman (Kalamazoo, MI: Cistercian Publications, 1995), XV. 39.

83. Vacek, *Love, Human and Divine,* 258.

84. Ibid., 271.

85. Ibid., 157–58.

86. Ibid., xvi.

87. Ibid., 280–81.

88. Ibid., 309.

89. Vacek, *Love, Human and Divine,* 224, emphasis in original.

90. Paul Wadell and Patricia Lamoureux, *The Christian Moral Life: Faithful Discipleship for a Global Society* (Maryknoll, NY: Orbis Books, 2010), 201.

91. I take this to be a point in Pope Benedict's understanding of love. See Benedict XVI, *Deus caritas est,* nos. 5–6.

92. Ibid., no. 7.

93. Ibid., no. 10.

94. Ibid., no. 43.

95. For example, Matthew 22:34–40, Mark 12:28–34, and Luke 10:25–28. John 13:34–35, Galatians 5:14, and 1 John 3:23 command us to love our neighbor.

96. Bruce Birch, "Justice," in *Dictionary of Scripture and Ethics.* ed. Joel Green (Grand Rapids, MI: Baker Academic, 2011).

97. Thomas Aquinas, *Summa Theologica*, II–II, Q. 58

Chapter 4: Actions and Persons

1. John Paul II, *Veritatis Splendor*, no. 78.

2. Richard Gula, *Reason Informed by Faith: Foundations of Catholic Morality* (New York: Paulist Press, 1989), 267.

3. Kaye Gibbons, *A Virtuous Woman* (New York: Vintage Contemporaries, 1989), 8.

4. Gula, *Reason Informed by Faith,* 267.

5. *Catechism of the Catholic Church,* no. 1754.

6. Gula, *Reason Informed by Faith*, 266.

7. John Paul II, *Veritatis Splendor*, no. 78.

8. *Catechism*, no. 1735.

9. James Keenan, *A History of Catholic Moral Theology in the Twentieth Century: From Confessing Sins to Liberation Consciences* (New York: Continuum, 2010), 185.

10. Ibid., 184.

11. For a short discussion of this see Pontifical Biblical Commission, *The Bible and Morality: Biblical Roots of Christian Conduct,* no. 83.

12. John Paul II, *Veritatis Splendor*, no. 80. Note that the Pope makes a significant moral claim here. While he refers to these as intrinisically evil, his source, the Second Vatican Council, refers to these as "supreme dishonor to the Creator."

13. Second Vatican Council, *Gaudium et Spes*, no. 29. These acts are "contrary to God's intent."

14. John Paul II, *Veritatis Splendor*, no. 80.

15. See *Catechism of the Catholic Church*, no. 1756 and no. 2357.

16. See National Conference of Catholic Bishops, *The Challenge of Peace: God's Promise and Our Response* (Washington, DC: United States Catholic Conference, 1983), nos.142–61.

17. Pontifical Council for Justice and Peace, *Compendium of the Social Doctrine of the Church,* no. 497.

18. American Lung Association, www.lungusa.org/stop-smoking/about-smoking/health-effects/smoking.html.

19. John Mahoney, *The Making of Moral Theology: A Study in the Roman Catholic Tradition* (Oxford: Clarendon Press, 1989), 312.

20. Gula, *Reason Informed by Faith*, 268.

21. John Paul II, *Veritatis Splendor*, no. 80.

22. United States Conference of Catholic Bishops, *Forming Consciences for Faithful Citizenship: A Call to Political Responsibility from the Catholic Bishops of the United States*, nos. 22, 23.

23. William Frankena, *Ethics* (Englewood Cliffs, NJ: Prentice Hall, 1973), 87–88.

24. Ibid., 89.

25. John Paul II, *Veritatis Splendor*, no. 80.

26. William Cavanaugh, *Being Consumed: Economics and Christian Desire* (Grand Rapids, MI: Wm. B.Eerdmans, 2008), 41.

27. Cathleen Kaveny, *Law's Virtues: Fostering Autonomy and Solidarity in American Society* (Washington, DC: Georgetown University Press, 2012), 233.

28. Ibid., 236.

29. Ibid., 11.

30. See ibid., chapters 9 and 10.

31. Joseph Mangan, "An Historical Analysis of the Principle of the Double Effect," *Theological Studies* 10, no. 1 (March 1949): 41–61.

32. See Augustine, *On Free Choice of the Will,* trans. Anna Benjamin and L. Hackstaff (Indianapolis: Bobbs-Merill Educational Publishing, 1981). Bk. 1, chaps. 3–6.

33. Thomas Aquinas, *Summa Theologica* II-II, Q.64, Art.7, trans. Mangan in "An Historical Analysis of the Principle of the Double Effect," 44.

34. Ibid., 61.

35. Ibid., 43.

36. Ibid., 41.

37. Ibid., 60.

38. Sissela Bok, *Lying: Moral Choice in Public and Private Life* (New York: Vintage Books, 1989), 15.

39. For example, Bernard Gert, *Morality: A New Justification for Moral Rules* (Oxford: Oxford University Press, 1988).

40. See Bok, *Lying*, chaps. 5–15.

41. Kaveny, *Law's Virtues*, 224.

42. Ibid.

43. Ibid.

44. Darlene Fozard Weaver, *The Acting Person and Christian Moral Life* (Washington, DC: Georgetown University Press, 2011), 52.

45. *Catechism of the Catholic Church*, no. 850.

46. Gary Anderson, *Sin: A History* (New Haven: Yale University Press, 2009), 13.

47. Ibid., 54.

48. Ibid.

49. Weaver, *The Acting Person and Christian Moral Life*, 52.

50. Ibid., 43.

51. Pontifical Biblical Commission, *The Bible and Morality,* no. 81.

52. Ibid.

53. See John Paul II, *Sollicitudo Rei Socialis*, no. 36.

54. Martin Luther King Jr., "Letter from Birmingham City Jail," in *A Testament of Hope: The Essential Writings and Speeches of Martin Luther King Jr.*, ed. James Washington (San Franciso: HarperSanFranciso, 1991), 296.

55. Ibid., 295.

56. Aquinas, *Summa theologica*, II-II, Q. 24, Art. 10.

57. See Weaver, *The Acting Person and Christian Moral Life*, 156–58.

58. Ibid., 168 (italics in the original).

59. Aquinas, *Summa theologica*, II-II, Q. 24, Art. 2.

60. Pontifical Biblical Commission, *The Bible and Morality*, no. 81

Chapter 5: Conscience

1. Mark Twain, *Adventures of Huckleberry Finn* (New York: Harper & Brothers, 1912), 285.

2. Richard Gula, *Reason Informed by Faith: Foundations of Catholic Morality* (Mahwah, NJ: Paulist Press, 1989), 123.

3. There are great debates among philosophers and biologists about the relation between the mind, mental activity, the brain, and the functioning of our central nervous system. These debates are, thankfully, beyond the scope of this work.

4. Darlene Fozard Weaver, "Conscience: Rightly Formed and Otherwise," *Commonweal*, September 23, 2005.

5. Gula, *Reason Informed by Faith*, 124.

6. Ibid.

7. Joseph Ratzinger, *On Conscience* (San Francisco, CA: Ignatius Press, 2007), 26.

8. Gula, *Reason Informed by Faith*, 124.

9. Steven Pinker, "The Moral Instinct," *New York Times Magazine*, January 13, 2008, 37. He writes, "People everywhere, at least in some circumstances and with certain other folks in mind, think it's bad to harm others and good to help them. They have a sense of fairness: that one should reciprocate favors, reward benefactors and punish cheaters. They value loyalty to a group, sharing and solidarity among its members and conformity to its norms. They believe that it is right to defer to legitimate authorities and to respect people with high status. And they exalt purity, cleanliness and sanctity while loathing defilement, contamination and carnality," 36.

10. Ibid., 56.

11. John Mahoney, *The Making of Moral Theology: A Study of the Roman Catholic Tradition* (Oxford: Clarendon Press, 1987), 290.

12. Robert Hare, *Without Conscience: The Disturbing World of the Psychopaths Among Us* (New York: Guilford Press, 1999), xi.

13. Elie Wiesel, "Without Conscience," *New England Journal of Medicine* 352, no. 15 (April 14, 2005): 1511.

14. Ibid., 1512.

15. Ibid., 1513.

16. Bryan Massingale, *Racial Justice and the Catholic Church* (Maryknoll, NY: Orbis Books, 2010), 115.

17. Ibid.

18. The Second Vatican Council, *Gaudium et Spes*, no. 1.

19. Ibid., 117.

20. John Paul II, *Sollicitudo Rei Socialis*, no. 38.

21. Ibid., no. 40.

22. This discussion of conscience is informed by the *Catechism of the Catholic Church* as well as the work of Richard Gula, *Reason Informed by Faith* and *Moral Discernment* (Mahwah, NJ: Paulist Press, 1997); Russell Connors and Patrick McCormick, *Character, Choices and Community: The Three Faces of Christian Ethics* (Mahwah, NJ: Paulist Press, 1998); John Neafsey, *A Sacred Voice Is Calling: Personal Vocation and Social Conscience* (Maryknoll, NY: Orbis Books, 2006); Paul Wadell, *Happiness and the Christian Moral Life: An Introduction to Christian Ethics* (Lanham, MD: Rowman and Littlefield, 2008); Charles Curran, *The Catholic Moral Tradition Today* (Washington, DC: Georgetown University Press, 1999); and James Martin, *The Jesuit Guide to (Almost) Everything: A Spirituality for Real Life* (New York: HarperOne, 2010).

23. Franz Bockle, *Fundamental Concepts of Moral Theology* (New York: Paulist Press, 1968), 70.

24. Curran, *The Catholic Moral Tradition Today*, 186.

25. Neafsey, *A Sacred Voice is Calling*, 137.

26. Martin, *The Jesuit Guide to (Almost) Everything*, 313.

27. Thomas Aquinas, *Summa Theologica*, II-II, Q. (New York: Benziger Brothers, 1947), 47–56.

28. Martin, *The Jesuit Guide to (Almost) Everything*, 306.

29. Ibid., 325.

30. Ibid., chap. 12.

31. Ibid., 316.

32. James Gustafson, *Ethics from a Theocentric Perspective*, vol. 1,C *Theology and Ethics* (Chicago: University of Chicago Press, 1981), 338.

33. Kevin O'Rouke, "From Intuition to Moral Principle," *America Magazine* 203, no. 14 (November 15, 2010): 12.

34. See Richard Gula, *Moral Discernment*.

35. See Aquinas, *Summa Theologica*, II-II, Q. 47.8.

36. Joseph Fitzmyer, "Pauline Theology," in *The New Jerome Biblical Commentary*, ed. Raymond Brown, Joseph Fitzmyer, Roland Murphy (Englewood Cliffs, NJ: Prentice Hall, 1990), 1414. The word "conscience," the Latin translation of the Greek work *syneidesis*, appears thirty times in the New Testament (and once in the Old Testament). It does not appear in the Gospels; all but two of the thirty instances appear in the letters attributed to St. Paul.

37. See Second Vatican Council, *Lumen Gentium*, no. 25.

38. United States Conference of Catholic Bishops, *National Directory for Catechesis* (Washington, DC: United States Conference of Catholic Bishops Publishing, 2005), 165.

39. Mahoney, *The Making of Moral Theology*, 291.

40. *Catechism of the Catholic Church*, no. 1776.

41. Lawrence Boadt, "Ezekiel," in T*he New Jerome Biblical Commentary*, ed. Brown, Fitzmyer, and Murphy, 325.

42. Heinz-Josef Fabry, "leb" in *Theological Dictionary of the Old Testament*, vol. 7, ed. G. Johannes Botterweck, Helmer Ringgren, and Heinz-Josef Fabry (Grand Rapids, MI: Wm. B. Eerdmans, 1995), 419.

43. For example, "Heart," in *The Oxford Dictionary of the Christian Church*, ed. F. L. Cross (Oxford: Oxford University Press, 1990), 623. And John McKenzie, "Aspects of Old Testament Thought," in *The New Jerome Biblical Commentary*, ed. Brown, Fitzmyer, Murphy, 1305.

44. *Catechism of the Catholic Church*, no. 1776.

45. John Paul II, *Veritatis Splendor*, no. 58.

46. *Catechism of the Catholic Church*, no. 2562

47. John Paul II, *Veritatis Splendor*, no. 58.

48. Augustine, *Confessions*, trans. Maria Boulding (New York: New City Press, 1997), Book 10, sec. 8, 9. Augustine describes this as taking place in the "mind."

49. Charles Taylor, *Sources of the Self: The Making of the Modern Identity* (Cambridge, MA: Harvard University Press, 1989), 134.

50. Ibid., 132.

51. Ibid., 134.

52. Ibid., 135.

53. *Catechism of the Catholic Church*, no. 1779.

54. Thomas Merton, Naomi Stone, and Patrick Hart, ed., *Loving and Living* (New York: Farrar Straus Giroux, 1979), 40, 41.

55. Mother Teresa, quoted in *Modern Spiritual Masters: Writings of Contemplation and Compassion,* ed. Robert Ellsberg (Maryknoll, NY: Orbis Books, 2008), 26.

56. Martin, *The Jesuit Guide to (Almost) Everything*, 141.

57. Ibid., chapter 4. Martin describes three forms of the examen: the original, written by St. Ignatius and found in his *Spiritual Exercises*, one practiced by Dorothy Day, and the third is his interpretation. The one mentioned in this text combines the three, hopefully in the spirit of the tradition.

58. See Pontifical Biblical Commission, *The Bible and Morality: Biblical Roots of Christian Conduct,* nos. 77–79.

59. Ibid., no. 20.

60. *Catechism of the Catholic Church*, no. 2563.

61. Ibid., no. 1784.

Index